JESUS THE O

This study course has been published by Monarch in cooperation with

TIME MINISTRIES INTERNATIONAL

TIME encourages unity within a local church (of any denomination) for every member ministry and mission.

TIME aims that the local church should be:

> **T**ogether for
> **I**ntercession,
> **M**inistry and
> **E**vangelism.

The study course *Called to Serve*, which has sold nearly 20,000 copies and is used by hundreds of churches world-wide, is an invaluable foundation course for church leaders and members. It deals with what it means to be a disciple of Christ and what in practice it means for the local church to be the body of Christ, according to Scripture.

Called to Serve is available, together with essential leader's resources about the TIME strategy for church development or church planting from:

Emmanuel Church, Main Road, Hawkwell, Hockley, Essex S55 4NR. (Telephone 0702 205865; Fax 0702 207753)

TONY & PATRICIA HIGTON

JESUS THE ONLY SAVIOUR

A WORKBOOK ON **CHRISTIANITY** & OTHER FAITHS

MONARCH
Tunbridge Wells

Copyright © Tony and Patricia Higton
The right of Tony and Patricia Higton to be identified
as authors of this work has been asserted by them in
accordance with the Copyright, Design
and Patents Act 1988.

First published 1993

All rights reserved.
No part of this publication may be reproduced or
transmitted in any form or by any means, electronic
or mechanical, including photocopy, recording, or any
information storage and retrieval system, without
permission in writing from the publisher.

Unless otherwise indicated, biblical quotations are from the
New International Version.

ISBN 1 85424 222 9

British Library Cataloguing-in-Publication Data.
A catalogue record for this book is available
from the British Library.

Designed and Produced in England for
MONARCH PUBLICATIONS
PO Box 163, Tunbridge Wells, Kent TN3 0NZ by
Nuprint Ltd, Station Road, Harpenden, Herts AL5 4SE

CONTENTS

Introduction		9
1.	**What is God Like?**	13
2.	**Who is Jesus Christ?**	21
3.	**What is Salvation?**	37
4.	**Who is Saved?**	53
5.	**What about Other Religions? (Part 1)**	65
6.	**What about Other Religions? (Part 2)**	81
7.	**What about Idolatry?**	97
8.	**What about the Unevangelised?**	117
9.	**What about Interfaith Cooperation?**	141
10.	**How should we Respond?**	155
Appendix 1	**Exclusivism, Pluralism and Epistemology**	161
Appendix 2	**Malachi 1:11**	167
Appendix 3	**Outline of the Main World Faiths**	173
	Hinduism	173
	Buddhism	178
	Islam	183
	Judaism	188
	Differences between the Religions	192
Appendix 4	**Penal Substitution in Scripture**	195
Appendix 5	**1 Peter 3:19-20; 4:6**	209

Preface

This course is designed to be used not only by the individual but also by church home groups and Bible Study meetings.

Most sections are in two parts. The main part is Bible study for general use and includes suggestions for group discussion. The second part is 'For Further Study' and should be regarded as optional. This material is for those interested in a slightly more academic approach. There is also an Appendix which includes an outline of the major world religions and shows the fundamental incompatibility of their main truth claims. Again, this is optional material and some of it is for those interested in a more academic approach.

Although there are ten main sections it is likely that a study group would need up to twelve weeks to cover the material. This is without going into the 'For Further Study' sections.

INTRODUCTION

We live in a global village. In a little over a day we can travel to the far side of the world. Every country is readily accessible to the air traveller and holidays are possible in exotic corners of the world. Modern telecommunications bring the world into our living rooms. We can see life in any country and culture as it happens. And we can telephone across the world in a few seconds.

In politics and business, the world is interrelated. No nation can go it alone. The knock-on effect of local wars; the enormity of global problems; the immensity of multinational companies and the power of speculators on the international money-markets all require worldwide cooperation and potentially world government.

This century, with two horrific world wars culminating in the use of nuclear bombs, the trauma of the (nuclear) cold war and the growth of terrorism has understandably seen a growing desire for unity, harmony and peace.

The Interfaith Movement

Part of this desire has been manifested in the Interfaith Movement. So often, religion has created strife and even war, yet has great potential for good. It seems logical therefore to seek to bring the religions together to promote the welfare of the planet.

In 1893 a Parliament of the World's Religions was

held in Chicago. Never before had such a gathering taken place. It was seen as the beginning of the Interfaith Movement, with representatives from Buddhism, Hinduism, Islam, the Bahai faith and Christianity.

The World Congress of Faiths (WCF) was founded in 1936 by Sir Francis Younghusband to draw the faiths together in mutual understanding. Whilst in Tibet in 1903 he had a spiritual experience of the underlying unity of all beings (a belief central to Buddhism) and hoped the WCF could spread this experience.

In 1970 came the first meeting of the World Conference on Religion and Peace to encourage the leaders of the different faiths to cooperate in order to promote world peace.

In recent years most religious communities have formed organisations to promote dialogue and consultation with those of other faiths.

In 1986 Pope John Paul II invited leaders of other faiths to meet him in Assisi in Italy to pray together for peace. At about the same time the World Wide Fund for Nature (formerly World Wild-Life Fund) held a multi-faith gathering in Assisi to encourage the different faiths to cooperate for the sake of world conservation.

Since then the WWF has held controversial multi-faith services and events in various English cathedrals. In Winchester Cathedral in 1987 the 'Rainbow Covenant' was made between people of different faiths. 'The Prayer of Covenant' describes it as a covenant 'between us and God'. It was sealed by a Hindu ceremony.

In Canterbury Cathedral in 1989 a multi-faith liturgy totally excluded the name of Jesus.

In 1984 a multi-faith service in Newcastle Cathedral (not organised by WWF) included worship of Rama (the seventh incarnation of the Hindu god Vishnu). The words 'Lord Rama, King Rama, Lord of All, King

Rama, Lord Rama' were proclaimed. The name of Jesus was excluded from the liturgy.

The annual Commonwealth Day Observance in Westminster Abbey, in the presence of the Queen, has included Muslim, Sikh and Hindu worship. Also Buddhist and Hindu readings have affirmed salvation by works which, as we shall see, contradicts the Christian doctrine of salvation. The name of Jesus has been mentioned but readings from the Bible have been about moral teaching, not the person and work of Christ.

Different views of salvation

The main view throughout the history of the church is called:

The exclusivist view

This states that salvation is only through faith in Christ. Other religions are not salvific (ie, they do not bring salvation). At best they are a response to God's revelation in creation but contain much error. At worst they are totally wrong and demonic. Exclusivism is contrary to the spirit of the age and is often strongly criticised as arrogant, intolerant and unChristian.

During recent decades much more 'positive' views of other religions have developed within the church.

The inclusivist view

This states that God's supreme revelation is in Christ. Christ is the author of salvation and the norm by which all religious experience should be judged. However God is bringing people to salvation who do not know the name of Christ. They may be adherents of other religions. They are saved by Christ even though they do not have faith in Christ. This view is very attractive to modern ways of thinking.

The pluralist view

This view states that all religions are salvific. They teach different ideas of God based on different cultural and historical circumstances. Faith in Christ is merely one way of salvation.

(See the 'For Further Study' section for more information on these views.)

Growing antagonism to evangelizing other faiths

The growing influence of inclusivism and pluralism has led to increasing calls for Christians not to evangelize people of other faiths. Such evangelism is seen as unnecessary, arrogant and intolerant. It is also sometimes seen as racist because some religions are mainly associated with ethnic minorities.

The Decade of Evangelism has therefore proved very controversial among people of other faiths. Some church leaders have also sought to distance themselves from evangelism of other faith groups.

Because of this growing controversy and the fundamental importance of the subject, it is important that Christians look at what Scripture actually teaches. This course is offered as a resource to facilitate this.

[See Appendix 1 for information on Exclusivism, Pluralism and Epistemology.]

CHAPTER 1 | WHAT IS GOD LIKE?

One of our main concerns is to examine the relationship between the Christian faith and other religions. It is important therefore that we think about the nature of God, because our view of God governs what we believe about worship and salvation.

The Source of our Information about God

How can we know what God is like? It is generally accepted that love is the greatest human attribute, so it would be strange if God, who is by definition greater than mankind, were less loving than human beings. Rather we would expect him to be more loving, and that also means that he is personal.

It is, therefore, a reasonable assumption that God is *loving* and *personal*. Consequently we can expect him to communicate with us, for communication is central to love.

It is also a reasonable assumption that if God has something very important to communicate to us—like the way of salvation for human beings—he would communicate in a clear, permanent form. What better than a personal visit preceded and followed by written communication? Christians believe that God communicated in history through Jesus and gave us a clear, permanent record of that communication in the Bible.

So, given a personal, loving God, it is reasonable to expect written Scriptures. In this course we shall therefore take the Bible for our guide and authority, as the church has done over the centuries.

What the Bible Says

God is personal

Many people believe that God is an impersonal force, but the Bible teaches otherwise.

What is the most important evidence that God is personal?

John 14:9

God is loving

1. What does the apostle John say about God?

1 Jn 4:8,16

2. What do the following verses say about the love of God?

Ps 36:5,7

Jer 31:3

Jn 3:16

Rom 5:8

3. How does Psalm 86:15 describe God?

4. What characteristic of God is mentioned in the following passages?

Eph 2:7-9

WHAT IS GOD LIKE?

Tit 2:11

Grace is God's unmerited favour; its root meaning is 'giving pleasure'. Grace is always given, never earned. It is a relationship word not a 'force'.

Mercy is compassion shown to someone in need, in helpless distress, or in debt and without claim to favourable treatment.

The two words are similar but grace is concerned for man as guilty; mercy for man as miserable.

5. What is said of God's mercy in the following passages?

Eph 2:4

Mic 7:18

Is 55:7

God reveals himself

1. How does God reveal himself in the following passage?

Heb 1:1-3

2. What is the significance of the name given to Jesus in the following passage?

Jn 1:1,14

3. What does Jesus claim concerning himself?

Jn 12:45

Jn 14:7-9

God inspires Scripture

1. How was the Bible produced according to the following passages?

2 Tim 3:16

2 Pet 1:21

1 Peter 1:10-12 shows that the prophets did not always understand the message they were conveying concerning Christ.

Note that the writers are no mere 'human typewriters'. Sometimes they gathered material from other sources (see Luke 1:1-4); sometimes they described their own experiences as in many of the psalms, and the writers clearly have different styles. The Holy Spirit, without obliterating the writers' personalities, so overruled their weakness, sin and ignorance that what they wrote is reliable, true and authoritative. It is the Word of God.

2. How did Jesus regard the Old Testament?

Mt 5:17-19.

NB. Jesus credits to God words which were spoken by men in the Old Testament, eg Matthew 19:4-5 credits God with words spoken by the author of Genesis in chapter 2:24. Mark 12:36 says that David spoke Psalm 110:1 by the Holy Spirit. Also Acts 1:16 says that the Holy Spirit spoke Psalm 69:25 and 109:8 through the mouth of David.

The Bible clearly teaches that God is a personal, loving God. He is so loving that he is love. His infinite, eternal love embraces the world. He shows mercy and forgiveness to sinners. In his love he communicates with us. He reveals himself pre-eminently through Jesus. But he also inspired the writers of Scripture, which testifies about Jesus (John 5:39), so that what they freely wrote is God's Word.

But there is another important aspect to God's nature which will deeply affect our view of salvation and therefore of other faiths.

God is holy

This is shown in:

a. Purity

How do the following verses describe God's purity?

Mt 5:48

Deut 32:4

1 Jn 1:5

1 Tim 6:16

Heb 12:29

Hab 1:13 (1st sentence)

(See also Ex 15:11; Lev 19:2; Ps 18:30; Is 6:3; 1 Pet 1:15-16)

b. Wrath

1. Against what will God's wrath be shown according to the following verses?

Jn 3:36

Rom 1:18

Rom 2:8

Eph 5:6

Heb 10:26-31

2. How is God described?

Ex 34:14

3. What causes God to be jealous?

Ex 20:5

1 Cor 10:21-22

NB. The Bible often describes God in very human words which stress he is personal. (These words are called *anthropomorphisms* which literally means 'in the form of man').

Wrath and *Jealousy* are human words applied to God. With him they are not selfish, irrational passions, but are the reaction of his holiness against sin. It is a holy reaction. Our wrath and jealousy are often anything but holy.

See the Appendix on 'Penal Substitution in Scripture' on p 195 for further information on the Wrath of God.

c. Justice

How does God judge?

Gen 18:25

Ps 96:13

Deut 11:26-28 (compare Gal 3:10)

All human ideals of justice are a pale reflection of God's perfect justice. How important it is that he treats each human being with absolute fairness, and that one day he will put right all the injustices of this world, including those perpetrated by men, governments and nations which are not corrected in this life.

The way of salvation must relate to the holiness, wrath and judgment of God as well as to his love, mercy and forgiveness. God longs to forgive but he would be unjust if he turned a blind eye to sin, including the sin of ignoring or rejecting his revelation through his son. We shall return to this dilemma in Section 4.

GROUP DISCUSSION

It is possible for any one of us to make God in our own image rather than to have a biblical view of God.

Discuss ways in which your view of God may be unbalanced compared with the biblical description which you have just studied.

CHAPTER 2 | WHO IS JESUS CHRIST?

It is clear from the New Testament and from church history that this question has been a major source of controversy since the time of the apostles. Jesus himself confronted Peter with it in Matthew 16:13. He asked, 'Who do people say the Son of Man is?' The disciples replied, 'Some say John the Baptist; others say Elijah; and still others, Jeremiah or one of the prophets.'

In other words the general opinion was that Jesus was a prophet, maybe a great prophet, but merely a prophet. Many would take the same view today, some of them, sadly, in the nominal Christian church. Those of other faiths and even those of no faith would agree. His moral and spiritual teaching is widely respected. Such a Jesus would fit well into our modern multi-faith world.

The person of Jesus is fundamental to Christianity. We must therefore address the question of who he is. So we shall look back at how the apostles viewed him.

The disciples would not have thought that a human being could be divine[1]

The disciples, as Jews, would have been strict monotheists ['Monotheism' is the belief that there is only one God.]

Write out the words of the Jewish creed, called the *Shema* (pronounced 'shumah' with emphasis on the 'ah') after the Hebrew for the first word 'Hear'. Jesus quotes them in:

Mk 12:29

22 JESUS THE ONLY SAVIOUR

This statement is still made at the beginning of every synagogue service.

However impressed the disciples were with Jesus they would never have anticipated that he was divine. To them the idea that a human being could be divine would have been a blasphemous heresy.

For many months the disciples regarded Jesus as a teacher with miraculous powers or as the latest in the line of great prophets or eventually as the Messiah. (In their view the Messiah may have had supernatural powers but he was not divine.)

Some exalted statements were made at the beginning of his ministry

1. What did John the Baptist say of Jesus?

Mt 3:11-12

2. How did God describe Jesus at his baptism?

Mt 3:16-17

3. What else did John the Baptist say to the crowds about Jesus?

Jn 1:29

Jn 1:34

4. What did the disciples call Jesus the day after John the Baptist recognised him?

Jn 1:38

Jn 1:41

WHO IS JESUS CHRIST? 23

5. What did Nathaniel call Jesus on the following day?

Jn 1:49

But did the disciples fully understand these descriptions?

1. What was John the Baptist's reaction?

Mt 11:3

2. What was Jesus' family's reaction?

Mk 3:21

3. What was the disciples' reaction in the following passages?

Mt 8:27

Lk 24:19-24

Mt 28:17

We have seen that God called Jesus his son at his baptism. Both John the Baptist and Nathaniel repeated this title. But later even John the Baptist had some doubts as to whether Jesus was the 'one who was to come'. The disciples also had doubts, some of them after his death or even after his resurrection.

Mary too, in spite of the events surrounding his birth, apparently shared the family's doubts about Jesus' sanity at one stage.

It appears that neither John the Baptist nor the disciples understood the full meaning of the title 'Son of God' as ascribing divinity to Jesus. Nor does it seem they understood the titles 'Lamb of God who takes away the sin of the world' or the one 'who will baptise with the Holy Spirit' as implying divinity.

Read 1 Peter 1:10-12. The prophets did not always understand the inspired messages they were conveying for the benefit of future generations.

In spite of some flashes of inspiration, the disciples grew slowly in their understanding of who Jesus was. Hence the importance of Peter's confession in Matthew 16:16-20. As we have seen, doubts even persisted after that.

The New Testament shows clearly that Jesus is human

The disciples had no doubts that he was human. But throughout church history there have been those who have doubted it. A heresy called Gnosticism flourished in the second century after Christ. It regarded matter as evil and so taught that God could never have united with a real human body. Therefore, Gnostics said, Jesus' body was not real.

The beginnings of it are found in the New Testament. Read 1 John 4:2-3 which is the clearest reference to it. But it is also behind Colossians 2:6-23; 1 Timothy 1:3-4; 6:3-5,20 and Jude.

If Jesus did not have a normal human body he couldn't have died for us and Christianity collapses. So it is important to look at the NT evidence for Jesus' humanity.

1. What normal human experiences does Jesus have in the following passages?

Lk 2:6-7

NB. It is important to remember that Jesus' birth was perfectly normal and natural. It was his conception which was miraculous.

Lk 2:40

Lk 4:2 (2nd sentence)

Jn 4:6

Lk 8:23 (1st sentence)

Jn 11:35

Lk 22:44

Jn 19:28

Jn 19:34

Jn 19:30

2. What does the risen Christ say to his disciples?

Lk 24:39

3. What very important difference in Jesus is described in the following passages?

Heb 4:15 (2nd half)

1 Pet 2:22

1 Jn 3:5 (2nd sentence)

But Jesus had miraculous powers

In the minds of these strict monotheists his humanity would have militated against any idea of his being divine. It was clear from the beginning, however, that he had supernatural powers. These were evidences that he was the Messiah (or Christ). When John the Baptist, in Matthew 11:3, asked if Jesus was 'the one who was to come', he meant the Messiah. Jesus replied by saying that his miracles were the evidence that he was the Messiah (Matthew 11:4-6). Isaiah had prophesied that the Messianic Servant would be a miracle worker (Isaiah 35:5-6; 42:7).

However, the miracles are not in themselves evidences that Jesus is divine.

1. How do the following passages say Jesus performed his miracles?

Lk 4:14-19

Mt 4:1

Acts 10:38

The New Testament stresses that Jesus did his miracles through the power of the Holy Spirit. Many scholars would say that, although he still had his own divine power as the Second Person of the Trinity, he chose not to use it during his life on earth.

2. What amazing statement was Jesus able to make because he did his miracles through the power of the Holy Spirit?

Jn 14:12

3. What works is he talking about (look at the context: verse 11)?

This shows that miracles in themselves do not prove the miracle-worker is divine.

Jesus made claims to divinity

Most of these quotations are from John's Gospel. Traditionally this is seen as the latest of the gospels (perhaps dating from AD 85). It is claimed that the more developed doctrine is evidence of longer reflection on eyewitness testimony. More recently scholars have suggested a date for John as early as AD 50 and not later than AD 70. They argue that the theology is not later but a different selection from that emphasized by the other (synoptic) gospels which influenced each other. John is seen as complementary to the synoptic gospels.

1. What does Jesus claim about himself?

Mt 28:18

2. What similar claim is in the following passages:

Jn 5:22,27

Jn 17:2 (cf.5:21)

3. What claim did some Jewish leaders accuse Jesus of making?

Jn 5:16-18

4. How did they react to this claim?

Jn 5:18

5. What claim did Jesus make in the following passages:

Jn 6:38 (cf v42)

Jn 6:39-40 (cf v51-58)

Jn 6:46

6. What claims does Jesus make in the following passages and how do some of the Jewish leaders react?

Lk 5:20-21

Jn 8:51-55

Jn 8:58-59

7. What does Jesus say of his relationship to the Father?

Jn 10:30

8. How do the Jews understand this claim?

Jn 10:33

How do they react?

Jn 10:31

9. What does Jesus claim for himself about a pre-existent life?

Jn 17:5

10. What does Jesus say of himself in the following passages?

Jn 6:35
Jn 8:12;9:5
Jn 10:7,9
Jn 10:11,14
Jn 11:25
Jn 14:6
Jn 15:1,5

In each case the 'I am' in the Greek is emphasised and cannot be dissociated from the divine name in the OT eg. Exodus 3:14, cf John 8:58.

We have seen that Jesus more than once is recognized by Jewish leaders as claiming to be God. They therefore attempt to execute him. He also claims that he lived before creation and that he alone has seen the Father. He states that all authority and judgment is committed to him. He has authority to forgive sins and to give eternal life to those who believe in him and keep his word.

(NB in John 14:28 Jesus says, 'The Father is greater than I'. In the context of John's Gospel this must be seen as referring to Jesus' voluntary submission to the Father in the incarnation.)

Post-Resurrection Statements about Jesus' Divinity

1. How does Thomas address Jesus?

Jn 20:28

2. What four things does John say about Jesus?

Jn 1:1,3

3. What do the following passages say about Jesus?

Phil 2:6 (1st phrase)

Col 2:9

Heb 1:3 (1st phrase)

1 Pet 3:22

4. What do the following passages call Jesus? (use the New International Version for this section)

Jn 1:18

Rom 9:5

Tit 2:13

Heb 1:8

2 Pet 1:1

(NB The NIV translation of all those passages, which states Christ's divinity clearly, is to be preferred to other versions like the RSV and AV in some cases, on academic grounds. See 'For Further Study')

Jesus commends Thomas for calling him 'my God', and the NT teaches that he is the eternal, divine Son of God, in his very nature God, the radiance of God's glory and exact representation of God's being. He is the agent and sustainer of creation. All the fulness of the deity dwells in him. He is our great God and saviour, God the one and only, who is over all.

GROUP ACTIVITY

We suggest that the group has a time of worship and prayer, praising God the Father for sending his son, who is both God and man.

Note (from page 21)

1. The only apparent exception to this would be a theophany, an appearance of God in human form. These took place at times in the Old Testament. But they were always very temporary and the figures manifested may not have been material. The Lord is said to have appeared to Abraham, Isaac and Jacob (Gen 12:7; 17:1; 26:2; Ex 6:3), although in Jacob's case this was a dream (Gen 28; 35:1,7). There sometimes seems to be an interchangeability between the Angel of the Lord and the Lord himself as in appearances to Abraham (Gen 18) and Gideon (Judg 6).

The Lord also 'appeared' in the burning bush (Ex 3) and the pillar of cloud (Num 11:25; 12:5; 14:10). Moses was allowed to see the Lord's 'back' (Ex 33:18-23). He also appeared to David (1 Chron 21:16-18) and to Solomon in a dream (1 Kings 3:5; 9:2).

FOR FURTHER STUDY

A. There are variant readings for the passages referred to in the last question above (all are referring to Christ).

a. John 1:18 is either 'God the one and only' or 'the only begotten Son'

According to Prof F F Bruce, *The Gospel of John* (Eerdmans: Michigan 1983), pp44f, the weight of the textual evidence from early manuscripts favours the former. Also this is an unparalleled reading and is therefore regarded as more likely. It would be unlikely that a scribe would have changed the latter into the former. In any case John is only repeating what he has said about the Logos in v 1.

b. Romans 9:5 is either 'Christ who is God over all' or 'Christ, who is over all. God be for ever praised!' or 'Christ. God who is over all be for ever praised!'

Prof C E B Cranfield, *International Critical Commentary 'Romans' Vol. 2* (T & T Clark: Edinburgh 1979), pp464ff, points out that the only argument in favour of the second and third alternatives is that, it is claimed, Paul does not elsewhere call Christ God.

However Cranfield adds that:
 i. Pauline doxologies refer to the person named in the previous sentence;
 ii. 'Praised' (*eulogetos* and its Hebrew equivalent *baruk*) is always the first word in an independent doxology in Scrip-

ture. Here it would not be if the second reading were adopted;

iii. Reference to Christ's 'human ancestry' suggests an antithesis will follow, ie about divinity;

iv. An independent doxology would be surprising in this context which speaks of the disobedience of the Jews.

v. The Greek naturally means 'Christ who is over all'.

vi. The Greek grammar does not support the translations 'God who is over all' or 'God who is blessed for ever'.

In addition Cranfield refers to the fact that:

i. Paul does apply to Christ OT passages which originally refer to Yahweh eg Rom 10:13.

ii. He accepts it is right to pray to Christ eg Rom 10:12-14.

iii. He associates Christ with God in a special way eg Rom 1:7.

iv. He refers to Christ as 'in the form of God' or 'in very nature God' in Phil 2:6.

Cranfield concludes (p468) 'it seems to us that the superiority of the case for taking v5b (of Rom 9) to refer to Christ is so overwhelming as to warrant the assertion that it is very nearly certain that it ought to be accepted.'

c. Titus 2:13 is either 'our great God and Saviour, Jesus Christ' or 'the great God and our saviour Jesus Christ'

Prof Gordon D Fee, *New International Biblical Commentary, 1 and 2 Timothy, Titus* (Hendricksons: Massachusetts 1984), p196, says:

i. A single definite article before 'great God' is best understood as controlling both nouns together.

ii. 'God and saviour' is normal terminology in the OT and Hellenistic religions.

iii. Nowhere else is the Father said to be joining the Son in the second coming. 'Appearing' is never used of God.

It seems likely therefore that the first alternative is the correct translation (so Dr D Guthrie, *Tyndale NT Commentary, The Pastoral Epistles*, 2nd edition [IVP: Leicester 1990], p212).

d. Hebrews 1:8 is either 'about the Son he says, "Your throne, O God..."' or 'God is your throne...'

Prof Harold W Attridge, *The Epistle to the Hebrews* (Fortress Press: Philadephia, 1989), p58, says that although 'God' is nominative, it is possible, even in classical Greek and common in the Septuagint and NT to use the nominative for the vocative. Jewish exegetes regularly understood the verse from the Psalm quoted (Psalm 45:6) as vocative. The writer to the Hebrews follows this tradition and addresses it to the Son. Clearly v9 is addressed to Christ.

Attridge points out that this interpretation is followed by most commentators including: F F Bruce, *The Epistle to the Hebrews; New International Commentary on the NT* (Eerdmans: Grand Rapids, 1964), p19; P E Hughes, *A Commentary on the Epistle to the Hebrews* (Eerdmans: Grand Rapids, 1977, p64; H Braun, *Qumran und das Neue Testament* (Mohr [Siebeck]: Tubingen, 1966), pp38-39; and A Vanhoye, *Situation du Christi: epitre aux Hebreux 1-2, Lectio Divina 58* (Cerf: Paris, 1969), pp176-177.

e. 2 Peter 1:1 is either 'our God and Saviour Jesus Christ' or 'our God and the Saviour Jesus Christ'.

Michael Green, *Tyndale NT Commentary, 2 Peter and Jude* (IVP: Leicester, 1987), pp68f, writes:

i. If 1 Peter 1:3 is translated 'the God and Father', this virtually identical phrase must be translated 'the God and saviour'.

ii. The other four places where Peter writes of 'our Lord and Saviour' (1:11; 2:20; 3:2,18) clearly refers to Jesus.

iii. When Peter wishes to distinguish the two Persons (eg 1:2) he uses a different construction.

He concludes, 'Probably, therefore, the author is calling Jesus God here.' (p69)

B. Philippians 2:6 says that Christ 'who, being in very nature God (literally 'in the form of God'), did not consider equality with God something to be grasped.'

Much has been written on this verse and P T O'Brien, *The Epistle to the Philippians* (Eerdmans: Michigan, 1991), pp207ff, comments on the various interpretations:

i. One interpretation is that 'form' (*morphe*) means essential attributes ie 'the essential nature and character of God'. (So F F Bruce, *Philippians* [Good News Commentary: San Francisco, 1983], pp45,51-52; J B Lightfoot, *St Paul's Epistle to the Philippians* [London, 1881], pp110,127-133)

But there is little evidence that Paul used the word in such a philosophical sense.

ii. Another view equates 'form' (*morphe*) of God with 'glory' (doxa), cf Heb 1:3 (So H A Meyer).

iii. Others equate *morphe* with 'image' (*eikon*) and draw a parallel between Christ the Second Adam and the first Adam made in the image of God. It is doubtful that this is true here.

iv. Still others interpret *morphe* as 'condition' or 'status'— but there is no such understanding of the word in Greek literature (so E Schweizer; R P Martin).

O'Brien concludes that *morphe* is that 'form which truly and fully expresses the being which underlies it'...'The expression does not refer simply to external appearance but pictures the pre-existent Christ as clothed in the garments of divine majesty and splendour' (pp210ff).

He defines the meaning of the phrase 'did not consider equality with God something to be grasped' as 'Jesus did not regard his equality with God as something to be used for his own advantage' (p215).

O'Brien quotes with approval N T Wright who comments, 'The pre-existent Son regarded equality with God not as excusing him from the task of (redemptive) suffering and death, but actually as uniquely qualifying him for that vocation.' (N T Wright *Arpagmos and the meaning of Philippians 2:5-11*, Journal of Theological Studies 37, [1986], p345). As O'Brien puts it, 'Divine equality meant sacrificial self-giving' (p216).

Prof R P Martin comments in Tyndale NT Commentaries, *Philippians* [Revised Edition], (IVP: Leicester, 1987), pp103f, 'In his pre-existent state Christ already had as his possession the unique dignity of his place within the Godhead. It was a vantage point from which he might have exploited his position and, by an assertion of right, have seized the glory and honour of the acknowledgement of his office.... The eternal Son of God... renounced what was his by right, and could actually have become his possession by the seizure of it, viz equality with God, and chose instead the way of obedient suffering as the pathway to Lordship.'

What does it mean that Christ 'made himself nothing' or 'emptied himself'. The old Kenotic Theory propounded that he gave up the *relative* attributes of deity—omniscience, omnipresence and omnipotence. There is no basis for such speculation in Philippians 2. And, as we have seen Jesus made claims of divinity during his earthly life. Also, linguistically 'in the image of God' cannot be the object of 'emptied' (*ekenosen*). Christ's self-emptying of himself was his taking the form of a slave.

H A Netland (*Dissonant Voices*, Apollos, Leicester 1991) pp146f points out that Professor C F D Moule of Cambridge argues conclusively that the evolutionary idea of NT Christology (a primitive low Christology gradually evolving by borrowing from extraneous sources into a high Christology) does not fit the data of the NT. He contends that some of the highest Christology is found in the Pauline epistles which are widely accepted as the earliest NT documents.

Netland (p147) then quotes Oscar Cullmann, 'Our investigation of the Christological utilization of *Kyrios*, *Logos*, and *Son of God* has already shown that on the basis of the Christological views connected with these titles the New Testament could designate Jesus as "God".... The fundamental answer to the question whether the New Testament teaches Christ's deity is therefore "Yes".'

CHAPTER 3 | WHAT IS SALVATION?

Before we can decide who can save us, we need to understand what we need to be saved *from*, and what we need to be saved *for*. The basic meaning of the word 'salvation' in Scripture is 'deliverance'. It includes deliverance from danger or evil.

Salvation as deliverance

1. From what does salvation deliver us according to the following passages?

Mt 1:21

Tit 2:13-14

Heb 2:14-15

1 Jn 3:8

Rom 5:9

Salvation includes deliverance from sin; from the fear and power of death; from the devil's power and God's wrath. But the root of the word 'salvation' in the OT is 'to be broad, spacious', ie to bring into a spacious environment. This illustrates the positive meaning of salvation.

2. What does Paul say about those who are saved?

Eph 1:3

Let us now examine the matter further.

Salvation as blessing

This includes being chosen, justified, united, reborn, sanctified and reconciled.

a. Chosen in Christ

In the OT the word 'elect' means a deliberate selecting after considering alternatives. In the NT it means 'to choose out for oneself'. The word 'predestinate', used only of God in the NT, means 'appointing a situation for a person' or 'a person for a situation'.

1. When did God choose us?

Eph 1:4

2. For what purpose did God choose us?

Eph 1:4

Rom 8:29

2 Thess 2:13

3. What attitude did God have to us when he chose us?

Eph 1:4

4. What did God predestine us to be?

Eph 1:5

b. Justified by Christ

1. What does the apostle John say about unbelievers?

Jn 3:18-19

2. Who has sinned?

Rom 3:23

3. Who is under a curse and why?

Gal 3:10
(See also Jas 2:10)

4. What is true for all of us?

2 Cor 5:10

Justification is a legal term meaning 'to acquit' or 'to declare righteous'. So the judge justifies (or acquits) the innocent (Deut 25:1). Some people wrongly justify the wicked (Prov 17:15). Witnesses may prove a person right or justify them (Is 43:9,26). In all these references the word used is 'justify'.

Justification, then, confers a legal status (being declared righteous or innocent), and cancels a legal liability.

5. Where does righteousness come from?

Rom 1:17

Rom 3:22

6. How is righteousness described?

Rom 5:17

7. How does it come to us?

Rom 3:22
Gal 3:8
Phil 3:9

8. What does God credit to people who have faith?

Rom 4:3,5,9
Gal 3:6

9. How does God justify us according to the following passages?

Rom 3:24
Rom 5:9
Gal 3:13
2 Cor 5:19

10. What happened to Jesus on the cross?

Mt 27:46

11. What is Jesus according to the following passages?

Rom 3:25
1 Jn 2:2
1 Jn 4:10
Mt 20:28

Mk 10:45

1 Tim 2:6

NB 'Blood' means the physical death of Jesus. 'Atonement' refers to human beings being made 'at one' with God or reconciled to God. 'Sacrifice of atonement' in the Greek is 'propitiation': it refers to appeasing God's wrath against sin.

The word 'for' which follows 'ransom' in the verses from Matthew and Mark is literally 'in exchange for'. Jesus was our substitute.

12. What happened to Jesus on the cross according to the following passages?

Is 53:4-6

1 Pet 2:24

On the cross Jesus, demonstrating the infinite love of God, bore our sins and the divine curse upon them. He was a ransom who died in exchange for us. Through his blood-sacrifice (a violent penal death) he appeased the wrath of God against human sin (he was a propitiation). He was our substitute who died our penal death (death as a punishment). Hence the term penal substitution or substitutionary atonement.

This is at the heart of the cross and therefore of the gospel. It is clearly taught in Scripture, but some people try to deny it or explain it away because they do not like the idea of the wrath of God against sin. It is contrary to the spirit of the age which, with its false, sentimental view of love, minimizes the seriousness of sin and cannot accept the idea of eternal punishment as consistent with a God of love.

See the Appendix on 'Penal Substitution in Scripture' on p.195

13. What did the cross achieve according to the following passages?

Rom 5:10-11

Rom 5:18-19

2 Cor 5:18-19

Eph 2:12-13

Col 1:19-22

14. What did God demonstrate on the cross?

Rom 3:25-26

15. Whom does God justify?

Rom 4:5

16. What are the results of justification according to the following passage?

Rom 8:1

(NB We are justified 'in Christ'—Gal 2:17—so Rom 8:1 is referring to justification.)

c. *United with Christ*

1. What does Isaiah say about the Lord?

Is 12:2 (First and last phrases)

This passage shows that salvation is not through the acceptance of a creed but through relationship with a person: the Lord.

2. How does the apostle Paul describe believers?

Rom 6:5

3. What is true of the person who unites himself with the Lord?

1 Cor 6:17

4. What are the benefits of being united with Christ according to the following passages?

Rom 6:5-6

2 Cor 5:17

Jn 15:5

Jn 15:7

5. What is the aim of spiritual growth?

Eph 4:15

Union with Christ is an intimate, vital and spiritual union with him and his people. It is through this union that we experience new life, strength, blessings and salvation. Like the soil to the plant so Christ is the source of all good things to us. Only as we remain in spiritual union with him do we enjoy these things. The inadequate human illustration of this union with Christ is the marriage relationship, which should be the deepest, richest and most satisfying personal human relationship we experience. It is an experience of surrender without absorption, of service without compulsion, of love without conditions.

d. Reborn in Christ

Regeneration is the act of God by which the principle of new life is implanted in man and the controlling influence of his life becomes the Holy Spirit. It is called new birth, being born again, being born from above. (Sadly, today there is a superficial use of 'born again' meaning politically right wing. This is not the biblical meaning).

1. What is our natural state just before God gives us new life, according to the following passages?

Eph 2:5

Col 2:13

This shows the necessity of supernatural new birth.

2. How important is the new birth?

Jn 3:3

3. What are the benefits of the new birth according to the following passages?

1 Jn 3:9

1 Jn 4:7

1 Jn 5:4

1 Pet 1:3

[NB. 1 Jn 3:9 refers to persistent and deliberate sin, not occasional lapses or sin through ignorance or weakness. The answer to such sin is in 1 Jn 1:9]

4. How is the new birth brought about, according to the following passages?

Jn 1:13

Jn 3:6,8

Jas 1:18

1 Pet 1:23

The new birth is to a new life, eternal life (Jn 3:15-16,36; 5:24 etc.)

5. What is eternal life?

Jn 17:3

e. Sanctified through Christ

1. What has happened to us through the sacrifice of Christ according to the following passages?

Heb 10:10

Heb 10:14

God sees the end result. Everything has been achieved by Jesus to make us perfect as ultimately we shall be.

1 Cor 6:11

2. What has Christ become?

1 Cor 1:30

God has declared those who are in Christ to be

already sanctified, holy and perfect. That is a legal (judicial) declaration. It shows how complete Christ's sacrifice is for us and how fully God accepts us even though we are sinners.

3. But what description of believers is found in the last six words of the following verse?

Heb 10:14

4. What is Paul's prayer?

1 Thess 5:23

Although God legally (judicially) regards us as sanctified (holy), in practical terms the Holy Spirit is in the process of making us sanctified (holy). A new recruit is legally regarded as a soldier, but his training is making him into a soldier in practice.

f. Reconciled in Christ

We are reconciled to God through the death of Christ (Rom 5:10; 2 Cor 5:18-19). But there is another vital element of reconciliation within salvation.

1. What was the main petition in Jesus' prayer the night he was betrayed?

Jn 17:11,21-23

2. How did this work out in the church at Pentecost?

Acts 4:32

3. Into what does the Holy Spirit baptise individual believers?

1 Cor 12:13

4. What was one purpose of the death of Christ, with respect to Jews and Gentiles, according to the following passages?

Eph 2:15b-16

Eph 3:6

(see also concerning male and female, slave and free in Gal 3:28)

5. What effect did God intend this to have?

Eph 3:10

6. What ultimate purpose does God have through the death of Christ, according to the following passages?

Col 1:20

Eph 1:10

NOTE 1. As we noted in the Introduction, this century has been the century of growing church and world unity. Part of this is cooperation between people of different faiths because religious extremism has often created violence and wars. Much of this cooperation is good. However, attempts to bring about *spiritual* unity between the faiths, eg. by multi-faith worship, are contrary to God's great purpose of bringing all things together under Christ. As we shall see later they tend to marginalize or even exclude Christ. Supernaturally, they are an attempt to sabotage God's purpose and create a false unity which is not under the Lordship of Christ.

NOTE 2. This is not, of course, an exhaustive study of salvation. It majors on individual salvation showing that any individual in Christ is a new creation (2 Cor 5:17).

7. What is God's purpose for the whole of creation according to the following passages?

Rom 8:19-21

2 Pet 3:10-13

Within this re-created universe those who are saved will experience not only the benefits listed in a—f above, but also complete wholeness in body, mind and spirit.

What must I do to be saved?

a. God takes the initiative

What is the ground of justification in the nature of God, according to the following passages?

Eph 2:8

Tit 2:11

Grace has been helpfully defined as an acrostic: '**G**od's **R**iches **A**t **C**hrist's **E**xpense'. It is God's kindness, unmerited favour, forgiving love.

b. The individual responds

What response does God look for in the individual according to the following passages?

Acts 16:29-31

Jn 6:40

Rom 10:9-10

Acts 2:38

NOTE 1. The place of Baptism

Christians agree that there must be a response of faith, repentance and baptism. However some believe they must be in this order. Others would allow baptism to come first, so long as the other elements follow on.

Water Baptism is clearly intended to accompany repentance, faith and reception of the Spirit. It is necessary as an act of obedience to Scripture. Hence we include it here. Some Christians would see it only as an outward sign. Others would say that, accompanied by repentance and faith, it is a means of receiving God's grace.

However, water baptism, as an outward rite, is not in itself a means of salvation. It does not, by itself, confer the supernatural experience of being spiritually baptised into Christ. This union with Christ is invisibly effected by grace through faith and visibly signified and sealed by baptism. (It is a fact of life that there are genuine Christians who, perhaps through the failing of their local church or their own negligence, have not been baptised. This should be remedied as soon as possible.)

NOTE 2. The place of keeping the law (keeping the Ten Commandments; living a 'good Christian life'; upholding New Testament standards)

i. Our salvation does not depend on 'good works'

What do the following passages say about the place of law-keeping in our justification before God?

Rom 3:28

Gal 2:15-16

Gal 3:11

Eph 2:8-9

ii. Our salvation will result in good works

James 2:24 says, 'You see that a person is justified by what he does and not by faith alone.' It has been said that this directly contradicts the teaching of Paul, and, on the face of it, this seems to be true.

However, the context of the verses, James 2:17-23, clarifies the matter. They stress that good deeds are an essential evidence of real faith. It is not possible to have real faith without showing it in good deeds. Some people claim to believe in Christ and be justified by faith, but their lack of good deeds shows they have not come to real faith. That means they have a mere intellectual belief. Such a faith cannot save anyone.

Paul is stressing that we cannot earn salvation by good deeds. Our good deeds are not good enough or sufficient in number. We would have to be perfect to be good enough for God. But because of his love, God sent his divine Son into the world to die for us, bearing our curse and condemnation. At that infinite cost Christ gained forgiveness and eternal life for us. God offers this forgiveness (justification) and eternal life as a free gift to all who really trust in him and his gospel.

James is concerned with religious hypocrites. He reminds us that if we have real, saving, justifying faith, it will show in good deeds. Without the evidence of good deeds it is clear we haven't got such faith. Paul hints at the same thing in Galatians 5:6 'The only thing that counts is faith expressing itself through love.'

Putting Paul and James together we can say this: **We**

are justified by the grace of God through faith in Christ and his cross, not because of any good deeds of ours. However, if we have such faith, and so are justified, it will show itself in the evidence of good works.

iii. We are saved by faith but judged by works (Rev 20:12-13). God will judge every man, woman and child perfectly. Those who trust in Christ will live with God eternally, but there will be complete fairness in the next life, according to how we have lived in this life. So it will be with those who have an eternity without God.

Just as the Bible talks about rewards for Christians (Eph 6:8), so there must be different degrees of judgment in hell. A just God will not mete out the same judgment to Hitler as a man who has lived a moral life but refused salvation through Christ. This teaching on salvation by faith but judgment by works is much neglected but makes much more sense of the concept of heaven and hell. If we choose to live without Christ in this life, we shall be without him in the next life. But there will be different degrees of reward and punishment in either heaven or hell.

Conclusion

It is clear that the NT teaches that salvation is in Christ. His death delivers us from sin, death and hell. God chooses us in Christ and in him we are justified, reconciled, reborn, re-created and sanctified. Through repentance and faith in Christ (sealed in baptism) we receive these blessings. The NT is Christo-centric (Christ-centred).

But is there salvation in anyone or anything else? Is Jesus the only Saviour? Is he the only way to God? We now turn our attention to these questions.

GROUP ACTIVITY

Share your testimonies of how you came to faith in Jesus as Saviour. If you have not yet come to faith, continue to seek the truth in the Bible, until you are able to pray this prayer from your heart:

Dear Father God, thank you that you love me;
Thank you that you sent your son to die,
bearing my sin and its penalty on the cross.
I turn away from my sin and put my trust in Jesus alone for my eternal salvation.
I gladly give myself back to you.
Strengthen me by your Spirit so that I might serve you for the rest of my life.

CHAPTER 4 | WHO IS SAVED?

Is Jesus the only way of salvation, the best way, or merely one way?

There are clear statements in the NT that Jesus is the *only* Saviour, the *only* way to God.

What did Jesus himself say on this matter?

Jn 14:6

What was the claim of the apostles after Pentecost?

Acts 4:12

(See 'For Further Study' Section)

Why is Jesus the only Saviour?

Is it simply because of the above statements? As we go through this section, we shall see that Jesus alone could be Saviour because of the very nature of God and the nature of human beings.

First, we remind ourselves of some of what we learnt about the nature of God in Section 2. We start from the basic principle that God is personal and capable of greater heights in personal relationships than human beings.

1. What does the apostle John say about God?

1 Jn 4:8

2. What do the following passages say about God?

Jn 12:48

Acts 17:30-31

Rom 2:16

Heb 12:23

(see also Heb 4:13; 9:27)

God is by nature love, the highest moral quality of personhood. He longs to bless human beings and the whole creation with the riches of his kindness and compassion. He is, however, by nature the judge of all humanity and will judge our sins one day. The standard will be his law.

3. What is Jesus' attitude to the law?

Mt 5:17-19

Christ has, of course, fulfilled the ceremonial law. But the moral law, summed up in the Ten Commandments, and explained in greater detail in the New Testament, must be obeyed.

4. How does God respond to sin (failing to keep his law) according to the following passages?

Rom 1:18-20

Rom 2:5-6

Eph 5:6

Col 3:6

God, because of the righteous wrath inherent in his

holy nature, will judge impenitent sinners. (Wrath does not mean bad temper.)

See also the Appendix on 'Penal Substitution in Scripture' on p.195).

5 (a) Where does God live?

   1 Tim 6:16

   (b) How does John describe God?

   1 Jn 1:5

   (c) What does John say about the Father and the Son?

   Jn 5:26

   (d) What does Jesus claim to be in both of the following passages?

   Jn 11:25
   Jn 14:6

   (e) What does God give?

   1 Tim 6:13

God therefore dwells in holy light and is alone the source of life.

6 (a) What prevents us having fellowship with God?

   1 Jn 1:6

(b) How does sinful humanity respond to the light of God?

Jn 3:19-20

Light and darkness cannot exist together in the same place. The light repels the darkness. So the light of God's nature repels the darkness of sin and, consequently, sinners.

(c) What does Paul say about 'the Gentiles'?

Eph 4:18

As God is by nature the source of life, when his light (purity) repels darkness (sinners) they are inevitably separated from that life.

(d) What is the result and penalty of sin according to the following passages?

Rom 5:12

Rom 6:23

Rom 8:13

The whole of humanity, by nature sinful, deserves a penal death (death as a punishment). The holiness and perfect justice of God's nature inevitably demands the death penalty for sinners. This death is spiritual (Eph 2:1,5) and, after this life, eternal separation from God (Lk 16:19-31; Mt 25:41; called 'the second death' in Rev 20:14-15)

Is there any way out? Could the death penalty somehow be transferred? Could God, in one and the same action, satisfy both his love (by saving humanity) and his justice (by punishing sin)?

Only a blood sacrifice deals with sin (Heb 9:22).

Clearly, sinful human beings cannot help: they stand condemned already. So only God who is perfect can help. If only God could somehow transfer humanity's death penalty to himself. His penal death would be infinitely more than equivalent spiritually to that of the whole of humanity.

7. What characteristic of God is affirmed in Paul's letter to Timothy?

1 Tim 1:17

1 Tim 6:15-16

So God cannot transfer the death penalty to himself because he cannot die. The only way of salvation for sinful humanity, therefore, would be if God could become man (without ceasing to be God) in order to suffer a penal death. *This is what he did in Christ, and only in Christ.*

8. How do the following passages describe the death of Jesus?

Mk 10:45

Gal 3:13

1 Tim 2:5-6

(NB. 'For many' in the Greek is 'in exchange for many'. Jesus is our substitute.)

2 Corinthians 5:14 states that 'one died for all, and therefore all died', ie. Christ's death (as both God and man) is equivalent to the death of all humanity. Hebrews 7:26-28 shows us that only Christ could be the perfect sacrifice, once for all.

See also the Appendix on 'Penal Substitution in Scripture' on p.195

To summarize the argument of the first four sections: Because of the very nature of God and the nature of sinful humanity, there could be no other way of salvation than for God to become man and die in our place. This has, of course, only happened in Jesus Christ.

SUMMARY

1. God is love.
2. He is also the judge of all mankind.
3. God's law must be obeyed.
4. Perfect justice demands that sin, which is the transgression of the law, must be punished.
5. God lives in unapproachable light and is alone the source of life.
6. Sinners therefore suffer eternal death (separation from God).
7. God alone can save mankind from sin and its consequences because he alone is free from sin and its condemnation.
8. If God could transfer humanity's eternal death penalty to himself, his penal death would be infinitely more than equivalent spiritually to that of the whole of humankind.
9. God cannot die: he is immortal.
10. So God must become man, without ceasing to be God, in order to suffer a penal death. HENCE, JESUS—HUMAN AND DIVINE, THE ONLY SAVIOUR.

The Resurrection

Although we are emphasizing Christ's penal death in this section, it is essential that we remember the fundamental place of his resurrection.

Christ bore the sins of the world and their curse. He experienced being forsaken by God on the cross. But when God raised him from the dead it proved he had not abandoned him to the grave (Acts 2:31; 13:37). It showed death could not keep a hold on him (Rom 6:9). In fact he was declared with power to be the Son of God through the resurrection (Rom 1:4). He is the author of life (Acts 3:15). Had he not been raised our faith would be in vain, we would still be guilty sinners and there would be no resurrection awaiting us (1 Cor 15:12, 14, 17).

But Jesus, who is the resurrection (John 11:25), has given us a living hope through his being raised (1 Peter 1:3). His resurrection is an assurance that we too shall rise from the dead (1 Cor 15:20).

He was raised to life for our justification (Rom 4:25) and we are saved by the supernatural power of his resurrection (1 Peter 3:21).

The apostolic preaching emphasized the resurrection (Acts 1:22; 4:2, 33; 17:31). According to their teaching salvation included a heart belief in the resurrection (Rom 10:9). It entailed knowing Christ and the power of his resurrection (Phil 3:10). It is described as being united with him in his resurrection (Rom 6:4-5; Col 2:12); being raised with him (Col 3:1).

Who is saved?

God is love and love desires a free response from the person loved. So God lays down repentance and faith in Jesus as a condition of receiving salvation.

1. How does John phrase it?

Jn 1:12

2. How does Paul phrase it?

Col 2:6

3. What is clear from the following passage?

1 Jn 5:12

4. What three things are said about the man who denies Christ?

1 Jn 2:22-23

5. What is said about the person who rejects the teaching of Christ?

2 Jn 9

So the only way to 'have' God is to trust in Jesus as the Christ and the Son of God incarnate.

6. How will true faith show itself?

Acts 20:21

As we saw in the Introduction, 'Inclusivists' believe that many who do not know about Christ will nevertheless be saved by him. But the Bible stresses the necessity of repentance and faith in Christ to salvation and it does not teach the 'inclusivist' view. However, we shall look at what the Bible says about the unevangelised (those who have never heard the gospel) in Section 8.

When are we saved?

Scripture teaches that believers *have been* saved (ie justification: see Eph 2:8 and Section 3); *are being* saved (ie sanctification: see 1 Cor 1:18); and *will be* saved: this refers to the consummation of our salvation, when we are finally accepted by God on the day of judgment and we experience wholeness in spirit, mind and body within the new heavens and new earth (Mt 10:22; Rom 5:9-10; Rom 8:23; 13:11; 1 Pet 1:5).

But is it possible for someone who dies as an unbeliever to be saved (justified etc) after death? Is there a second chance, an opportunity to come to faith, after death? Does the Bible teach this?

Here are some reasons why we cannot accept that this idea is biblical:

1. The story of the Rich Man and Lazarus (Lk 16:19-31).

Jesus makes it clear that there is no possibility of a second chance to be saved after death. The rich man was 'in agony' (vv.24-25) and knew that Lazarus was saved along with Abraham (vv.22-23). Abraham said to the rich man, 'Between us and you a great chasm has been fixed, so that those who want to go from here to you cannot, nor can anyone cross from there to us.' (v.26).

This story is often called a parable, which may be the case as it contains a fair amount of symbolism. If it is a parable, it is the only one where Jesus named one of the characters. Some say that Jesus is merely referring to commonly-held ideas without agreeing with them. However, it is very difficult to believe that Jesus would teach such a solemn lesson (about the impossibility of post-death repentance and the inevitability of eternal punishment for those who die impenitent) if it were not true. To do so would surely be a grave error.

2. Scripture teaches that ultimate acceptance by God is based on how we respond to Christ in this life.

Even those who call Jesus 'Lord' and perform miracles in his name but fail to do the will of the Father in this life will be turned away (Mt 7:21-23). Those who do not serve Christ in his followers in this life (see Section 6) will suffer eternal punishment (Mt 25:34-46). At his return Jesus will punish 'with everlasting destruction' those who 'do not know God and do not obey the gospel' in this life (2 Thess 1:8-9).

Scripture invariably teaches that final judgment will be based on things done in this life, never on the basis of things done in an intermediate state between death and the day of judgment. (See 'For Further Study').

GROUP ACTIVITY

Try to memorise an outline of the basis of our belief in Jesus as the only Saviour. One way is as follows:

In groups of 10, give to each member one of the points below, written on a piece of paper, numbered 1-10. Allow a minute to memorise that point. Then speak them out in order. If time allows, group members can be given another point to learn and speak out. In this way the basic reasons for our belief in Jesus as the only Saviour will be memorised.

The Ten Points

1. God is love.
2. God is the judge of all.
3. God's law must be obeyed.
4. A holy God must punish sin.
5. God is the source of life.
6. Sinners suffer eternal death.
7. Only a sinless God can save mankind by transferring the penalty of sin to himself.
8. The death of God would be equivalent to the death of humanity.
9. God is immortal and cannot die.
10. God became man to die in our place.

FOR FURTHER STUDY

John 14:6

Towards a Theology for Inter-Faith Dialogue, Board for Mission and Unity of the General Synod of the Church of England (CIO Publishing: London, 1984), p23f, comments on John 14:6, 'There is no suggestion in the context that Jesus is claiming to be "the whole of God", that outside him there is no truth to be found.' In Trinitarian doctrine it is true that Jesus is not 'the whole of God' and we do not deny that there are elements of truth in other faiths. But the report uses this argument to deny that the verse upholds 'a rigidly exclusivist view' of Christ. It is illuminating that, apart from quoting the whole verse, the report totally ignores the second half of the verse 'no-one comes to the Father, but by me'. That is 'rigidly exclusivist' and to ignore it is to be so prejudiced as to border on dishonesty.

Acts 4:12

Towards a Theology for Inter-Faith Dialogue comments (p23) 'the story is about healing and the authority by which this takes place.' The word 'saved' should, the report says, be translated 'cured' and 'salvation' translated 'healing'. It continues, 'It is going beyond the text to interpret it as a statement about other faiths.' But Peter is arguing in verses 10-11 that the healing is proof that Jesus was raised from the dead, the stone the builders rejected has become the capstone. The context is clearly *evangelistic*. It was this evangelism which got Peter and John in trouble with the Sanhedrin. The report's interpretation is an example of special pleading.

[For further information on 1 Peter 3:19-20; 4:6 see Appendix 5.]

CHAPTER 5 | # WHAT ABOUT OTHER RELIGIONS? Part 1

It is often assumed that all religious people worship the same God. But it is important that we carefully examine this fundamental issue.

In this Section we shall use 'Yahweh' as the generally-accepted name of the God and Father of our Lord Jesus Christ. The old form was 'Jehovah'. Hebrew had no vowels and the name of God was simply YHWH, which is from the verb 'to be', hence 'I AM'.

Are other religions reaching out to Yahweh?

Common Grace and Saving Grace

Some Christians so emphasise the *redemptive* work of God (salvation through Christ) that they almost ignore his *creative* work. Yet God put us in a beautiful world, full of a rich variety of colours and sounds. It ranges from the majesty of the mountains to the intricacy of the microscopic world. It is filled with thousands of different species of animals, birds, insects and plants, and is set in a universe of unimaginable size and splendour.

Then there are the achievements of humanity: music, art, literature, science and technology, to name but a few.

The Lord God created all this and sustains it. It

declares his glory. But it is much more than is strictly necessary to God's purpose of redemption or mankind's survival. It seems God delights in all this: he delights in blessing all his creatures.

1. How does God show this?

Gen 9:9-11

2. What remarkable aspect of God's love is described by Matthew?

Mt 5:44-45

God's blessings given to all humanity are often referred to as 'Common Grace'.

General Revelation and Special Revelation

Similarly, we must not so emphasize *Special* Revelation (the revelation through Christ and Scripture) that we underestimate *General* Revelation (through creation).

What do the following passages say about this?

Ps 19:1

Acts 17:25b-28

Rom 1:20

God therefore expects us to learn about his power, love and other qualities through creation. Furthermore, every human being is made in the image of God (Gen 1:26-27), and therefore will have some awareness of God, however dim it may be.

Down through the ages, and throughout the world, human beings instinctively try to worship God. We may conclude that other religions are partly a response to Yahweh's revelation in creation. As such they can contain genuine insights about him.

They have, in some cases, been influenced by special revelation too. This is obviously the case with Judaism (although it should be remembered that Judaism has moved a long way from the OT). Islam has also been influenced by biblical revelation but reacted against the divinity and atoning work of Jesus Christ.

However, it is certainly true that, even within the nominal church, people may follow false doctrines and myths (1 Tim 1:3-4), and even 'things taught by demons' (1 Tim 4:1). The same is true of other religions. Even a superficial glance at pre-Christian religions, tribal religions and some debased forms of Christianity will show that there may be a vague idea of a 'high God', but adherents concentrate on worshipping idols and appeasing spirits and demons. That does not mean we should think there can be no good theological and moral teaching in other religions.

The crucial question is whether other religions are salvific (ie bring salvation to their adherents). We saw in the last Section that the only way to 'have' God (ie. be saved) is to trust in Jesus as the Christ and Son of God incarnate. Other religions (whatever truth they contain) deny this truth and so are not salvific. In other words, many religious people reach out to the true God but do not come to know him through salvation in Christ, and therefore cannot worship him in spirit and in truth.

Does Christ work through all religions?

The Logos Teaching
Some people claim that the teaching on the 'Logos' (the Greek for 'Word') in John chapter 1 should make us

have an even more positive attitude to other religions.

Verse 9 says (referring to the Logos), 'The true light that gives light to every man was coming into the world.' 'Inclusivists' claim that this means Jesus (the Logos) is, often unnoticed and unacknowledged, bringing spiritual life and salvation to everyone on earth. He is said to be working in and through other religions to achieve this.

Adherents to this view agree that salvation is only through Jesus, but they claim that many are being saved through his work as the Logos, even though they do not realise it is Jesus, and therefore do not consciously respond in explicit faith in Jesus. So everyone is saved by the Logos (ie not through conscious faith in Jesus but by the secret work of Jesus as the Logos).

There is, of course, a moral problem here: there are millions of people who would not *want* to be saved by the Logos. But some proponents of this view appear to ignore the right of human free will to reject salvation by the Logos.

There is another problem with this view—the context of the verse. We have already seen that each human being will have some awareness of God, however dimly. But is this interpretation of John 1:9 really correct?

1. What is the light?

Jn 1:4

It is clear that the light is not some vague, secret spiritual illumination, but the life of the incarnate Son of God.

2. What is the reaction to the light?

Jn 1:5

Jn 1:10-11

Jn 3:19

Far from saving everyone, the light was rejected.

3. What does the light do?

Jn 3:20

4. Who are saved by the light according to the following passages?

Jn 1:12

Jn 12:46

(See Further Study Section on the Logos)

What is the attitude in Scripture to those not of Jewish/Christian Faith

It is increasingly being claimed that Scripture shows a positive attitude towards other faiths in the way that it deals with those not of the Jewish/Christian faith. We need to examine this matter carefully, in order to adopt a truly biblical attitude to other faiths. We shall look at the biblical passages commonly used to support these claims. In the rest of this section we look at:

Old Testament references.

Melchizedek

1. Who was Melchizedek?

Gen 14:18b

It is possible that Melchizedek was a Canaanite priest-king. The language he uses in blessing Abram in Genesis 14:19 is frequently used of the Canaanite chief deity—'most high', 'lord of heaven', 'creator of earth'.

2. Does Abram recognize the deity worshipped by Melchizedek as Yahweh?

Gen 14:22

However, the OT roundly condemned Canaanite religion. It involved polytheism (worship of many gods), child sacrifice and prostitution, although it may be that Melchizedek had risen above such practices, as he came to know about Yahweh.

3. What does the following passage imply about the reason for the later Israelite invasion of Canaan?

Gen 15:16

In view of the very negative attitude of the OT to Canaanite religion, even at the time of Abram, the story cannot be interpreted as approving of it. Rather Abram recognizes that Melchizedek has come to know Yahweh. There is no positive attitude to other religions here.

(For the relevance claimed for Abimelech, Jethro, Balaam, Ruth, The Queen of Sheba, the Widow of Zarephath, Job and Jonah, see For Further Study section.)

Naaman

Naaman was a Syrian who worshipped the God Rimmon.

1. What was Naaman's reaction to his miraculous healing according to the following passages?

2 Kings 5:15

2 Kings 5:17

This is a clear conversion to Yahweh.

2. What did Naaman ask for?

2 Kings 5:18

3. How did Elisha respond?

2 Kings 5:19

Some have argued that this story shows a positive attitude to other faiths and multi-faith worship. But all that Naaman asked for was forgiveness for a formal bow in the temple of a god in whom he no longer believed, because of his high position in Syria. The story does not justify a positive attitude to other faiths or multi-faith worship.

The Assyrians and Egyptians

In Isaiah 19:25 it says, 'The Lord Almighty will bless them saying, "Blessed be Egypt my people, Assyria my handiwork and Israel my inheritance".' Is God blessing Egyptian and Assyrian religion or accepting the Egyptians and Assyrians in spite of their religions? We must look at the context.

1. What does the whole passage prophesy?

Is 19:19

2. To whom do the Egyptians cry?

Is 19:20

3. What does Yahweh do?

Is 19:21

4. How do the Egyptians respond?

Is 19:21

It seems clear that this passage is foretelling a great turning to Yahweh by the Egyptians and the Assyrians (verses 23-24). Verse 25 should be read in the light of this. There is, again, no positive reaction to other faiths.

Cyrus
Cyrus, the pagan king of Persia, decreed that the Jews should return from exile to Israel.

1. How does God describe Cyrus in the following passages?

Is 44:28

Is 45:1

As we shall see, Yahweh called Nebuchadnezzar his servant too. The titles mean that these kings were used by Yahweh to serve his purpose.

Cyrus worshipped Marduk, the Babylonian high god. Some have claimed this is another name for Yahweh.

2. What does Yahweh say twice of Cyrus?

Is 45:4-5

3. What does Yahweh say of himself four times to Cyrus?

Is 45:5-6

Cyrus did not trust in Yahweh. Though he believed in the high god Marduk he did not thereby acknowledge Yahweh.
(See For Further Study on Cyrus.)

Nebuchadnezzar
Nebuchadnezzar was the pagan king of Babylon. Yet Yahweh called him his servant in Jeremiah 25:9; 27:6 and 43:10. After Daniel had interpreted his dream, Nebuchadnezzar affirmed Yahweh as 'God of gods and Lord of kings' (Dan 2:47). He went further and praised Yahweh as the Most High and King of heaven (Dan 4:32,34-35,37). This may not have been a full or permanent conversion. But there is no positive attitude towards other faiths whatsoever in this story. Nor is there a commendation of an incomplete conversion (if such it was).

Malachi 1:11
Some claim that this verse commends the worship of other faiths as acceptable to Yahweh. They translate it, 'My Name is great among the nations, from the rising to the setting of the sun. In every place incense and pure offerings are brought to my name because my name is great among the nations.'

The NIV (like the Authorised Version and the Revised Version margin) translates it as a prophetic future—so 'is' and 'are' become 'will be'. This translation makes it a prophecy of a time when the worship of

Yahweh will be worldwide. (The original Hebrew contains no verbs, so translators have to assess whether the writer intended the present or future tense.)

Appendix 2 is devoted to the different interpretations of this verse. A strong case can be made for it being irrelevant to other faiths. Certainly it is, to say the least, thoroughly unconvincing to base an important statement concerning the validity of the worship of other faiths on it.

CONCLUSION

In this section we have only been able to look at part of what the Bible says about other religions. But we might summarise what we have learnt in it by referring to the testimony of a prominent Anglican lay leader, known to the authors, who was once a zealous Hindu. He speaks of having been determined in his efforts to learn about God, but only when he became a Christian could he say that he knew God, and began to have a relationship with him which resulted in true worship.

GROUP DISCUSSION

In Section 8 we shall consider the matter of what happens to those who have never heard the gospel. But we have many opoortunities to spread the gospel. What are you and your church doing to spread the good news about Jesus to:

a. Your local area;
b. Your country;
c. The rest of the world (Acts 1:8)?

FOR FURTHER STUDY

THE LOGOS

Prof D. A. Carson, *The Gospel of John* (IVP: Leicester, 1991), p123f, says on John 1:9 that:

1. 'The verb *photizei* may mean "to illuminate (inwardly)" ie. "to give knowledge". Though lexically secondary, this meaning is common in the LXX...and is known in the NT.'

There are three possible interpretations:

a. General revelation cf. Rom.1:20 'But it is a little late in the Prologue to be harking back to that theme.'

b. The incarnation 'illuminating "every man" without distinction (ie not Jews only...)'. But the light has a more discriminating function.

c. Christ is the only light given to the world therefore he is the light for everyone (potentially). But the text does not say this.

2. The verb *photizei* has a primary meaning of 'to shed light upon', ie 'to make visible', 'to bring to light'. This is not inner illumination but an objective revelation, ie. the incarnation of the Word. It shines on every human being and divides humanity between those who reject it and those who accept it.

Dr J. H. Bernard, *International Critical Commentary, The Gospel according to John* (T & T Clark: Edinburgh, 1928), p12, comments: 'The Alexandrian theologians eg Clement, had much to say about the active operation of the pre-incarnate Word upon men's hearts; and it is interesting to observe that they did not appeal to this text, which is in fact not relevant to their thought as it speaks only of the universal enlightenment which was shed upon mankind after the Advent of Christ.'

C. K. Barrett, *The Gospel according to John* (SPCK: London, 1965), p134, commenting on John 1:9, states, 'When the Prologue is interpreted in terms of Hellenistic religion and the Logos thought of in a Stoic manner, it is natural to see in the present verse a reference to a general illumination of all men by the divine Reason, which was subsequently deepened by the more complete manifestation of the Logos in the incarnation....

'Whether John's words do in fact bear this meaning is, however, open to doubt. (i) In the next verse he emphasises that *'ho kosmos autou auk egno'* ('the world did not recognise him')—there was no natural and universal knowledge of the light. (ii) It was those who received Christ who received authority to become children of God. (iii) In the rest of the gospel the function of the light is judgment; when it shines, some come to it, others do not. It is not true that all men have a natural affinity with the light. In view of these facts it is well to understand *photizein* ("gives light") as... the light shines upon every man for judgment, to reveal what he is.'

Professor F. F. Bruce, *The Gospel of John* (Eerdmans: Michigan, 1983), pp35f, writes, 'It is from this true light that all genuine illumination proceeds. Whatever measure of truth men and women in all ages have apprehended has been derived from this source. Justin Martyr was not wrong when he affirmed that Socrates and the Stoics and others who had lived in conformity with right reason (logos) were really, if unconsciously, directed by the pre-existent Christ—although his use of logos was different from our Evangelist's. But the illumination that the Evangelist has primarily in mind is that spiritual illumination which dispels the darkness of sin and unbelief; and it was by coming into the world that the true light provided the supreme illumination—and provided it for all mankind. He is the light which enlightens every human being in the sense that the illumination which he has brought is for all without distinction.'

K. Cracknell, *Multi-Faith Worship?*, General Synod Board of Mission (Church House Publishing: London, 1992), paragraph 30, emphasises 'the independence of the eternal Logos or Word of God from the historical Jesus Christ, in whom the Logos fully dwelt for a period...the difference between the activity of God in Christ and in other human beings is cast as one of immeasurable degree, not of absolute kind.'

A very different interpretation from this seemingly adoptionist view, is given by J. A. T. Robinson, *The Priority of John* (SCM: London, 1985), p380. He writes, 'What I believe John is saying is that the Word, which was *theos* (1:1), God in his self-revelation and expression, *sarx egeneto* (1:14) was embodied totally in and as a human being, became a person, was personalised not just personified.'

OTHER OT CHARACTERS OFTEN CITED AS ILLUSTRATING A POSITIVE BIBLICAL ATTITUDE TO OTHER RELIGIONS

Abimelech

God speaks to Abimelech, King of Gerar, through a dream in Gen 20:3-7. This was a warning that Abraham had deceived him by saying Sarah was his sister, not his wife. His innocent intention to take Sarah as his wife would have incurred divine judgment, especially as she was to be the mother of the promised son of Abraham. But this act of mercy only shows that God can speak to people outside the covenant community. It does not show any positive attitude to other religions.

Jethro

Jethro was a priest of Midian who came to believe that Yahweh was greater than all other gods.

Some people have used him as an example of approval in the OT of people not being fully converted to Yahweh, but merely accepting that he is the true God, whilst remaining in their own religious context. However there is no commendation of such a position here, even if it is the position Jethro adopts, which is uncertain.

Balaam

Balaam was a pagan diviner of international reputation. Moab was so afraid of Israel invading her that the leaders enlisted Balaam's services to curse Israel. Yahweh then spoke to Balaam forbidding him to curse Israel (Num 22:12). He refers to 'Yahweh, my God' in verse 18. It may be that Balaam was taken aback by Yahweh's response when he normally dealt with unreal, so-called deities.

Yahweh then gave Balaam prophetic messages (Num 23-24). Whether he was genuinely converted to Yahweh is open to debate. But there is no positive attitude to other religions whatsoever in this story.

(Deut 4:19; 29:26 need to be considered. However we shall examine these in Section 7 'What about Idolatry?')

Ruth
Ruth has been used to support the idea that the OT is positive towards other faiths. But, although originally a Moabitess, she came to believe in Yahweh (Ruth 1:16). There is no positive attitude to other faiths here, but rather a conversion from another faith.

The Queen of Sheba
Even the Queen of Sheba has been recruited to support the theory of a positive biblical attitude to other faiths. She certainly saw that Solomon's greatness was the result of Yahweh's love for Israel (1 Kings 10:9). She was commended for coming to learn from Solomon's God-given wisdom (Mt 12:42), but there is no evidence she came to faith in Yahweh. However there is no positive attitude to other religions in this story.

The Widow of Zarepheth
Although from a pagan nation, God had told her to look after Elijah and she benefited from miraculous provision through him (1 Kings 17:9-24). Again there is no positive attitude to other religions here.

Job
Job was an Edomite but the book shows he was a definite believer in Yahweh. There is no evidence of a positive attitude to other religions.

Cyrus (additional material)
Claus Westerman, *Isaiah 40-66:A Commentary* (SCM: London, 1969), pp160f, says,'The repetition of the words "though you do not know me" underlines their importance... Yahweh's actions through the agency of his anointed

certainly do not form the beginning of any permanent relationship. This in itself shows that, contrary to the view of a large number of editors, in particular Volz, Deutero-Isaiah has no idea that Cyrus was to be converted and become a servant of Yahweh. Instead the present passage is the express statement that this will not be true.'

The Sailors in Jonah's Boat

Even these pagan sailors have been used as evidence that the OT did not require complete conversion from other faiths. But these men appeared to remain polytheistic (although their polytheism included Yahweh) and they are certainly not commended. So this story is irrelevant to a discussion of other faiths.

The People of Nineveh

Yahweh sent Jonah to prophesy against the sins of pagan Nineveh. He did so successfully and the city repented (Jon 3). God forgave them. Luke 11:32 commends Nineveh for repenting. But there is nothing commending a positive attitude to other religions in this story.

CHAPTER 6

WHAT ABOUT OTHER RELIGIONS?
Part 2

What is the Attitude of the New Testament to other Religions?

In this chapter we look at the NT references which some claim show a positive attitude to other faiths.

The Magi

This story (Mt 2:1-12) shows that God gave a partial revelation about the birth of Christ to non-Jewish astrologers. He met them on their own ground but they needed biblical revelation (verses 2-6) to complete their search. This is an example of God going beyond general revelation with those outside the covenant community. However there is no commendation of their astrology or religion.

(For material on the Canaanite woman Mt 15:22ff, see For Further Study.)

The Sheep and the Goats

This parable seems to suggest that people who unwittingly serve Christ by serving their fellow-men will receive eternal life (Mt 25:34-40). This could, of course, be applied to people of other faiths.

Is this passage teaching justification by works? Some interpreters say it is; others say that the word 'brothers' in verse 40 refers to Jesus' disciples, not needy people in general and this seems much more likely. If this is the case then Jesus is commending those who show their faith and love for him by serving his disciples. They have eternal life.

The reasons for favouring this latter interpretation are as follows:

i. In verse 40 the phrase Jesus uses is 'Whatever you did for one of the least of these brothers of mine, you did for me.' A similar passage is Matthew 10:40-42 where Jesus says to his *disciples*, 'He who receives you receives me.' He continues that anyone who receives a prophet (or righteous man) because he is a prophet (or righteous man) will receive a prophet's (or righteous man's) reward. Finally, he adds, 'if anyone gives even a cup of cold water to one of these little ones *because he is my disciple*, I tell you the truth, he will certainly not lose his reward.'

ii. The term 'little ones' in Matthew 10:42 probably refers to adult disciples, not just children. It is parallel to 'the least of these brothers of mine' in Matthew 25:40. (The For Further Study section quotes scholars who support the view that Jesus was referring to *disciples*, not humanity in general in Matthew 25:40.)

Who is Jesus referring to in the only other passages where he speaks of family members or 'brothers'?

Mt 12:46-50

Mt 23:8-9

Mt 28:10 (cf v16)

Jn 20:17

These passages further support the interpretation of 'brothers' in Matthew 25:40 as meaning disciples.

Also Matthew's Gospel makes it clear that salvation

is through the death of Christ, not by mere humanitarian action. He gave his life 'as a ransom for many' (20:28). This is confirmed by the Words of Institution of Communion, 'this is my body...this is my blood of the covenant, which is poured out for many for the forgiveness of sins' (26:26,28). And the Gospel also stresses the centrality of whole-hearted commitment to Christ (8:22; 10:32f,37f; 19:29).

The Samaritan Woman

Who were the Samaritans? We need to look back at Old Testament history. The Assyrians had resettled foreigners into the land of Israel during the Jewish exile (2 Kings 17:24). Each national group resettled there worshipped its own gods and consequently experienced divine judgment. So Assyria arranged for them to be taught how to worship Yahweh as well as their own gods (2 Kings 17:25-41). There was intermarriage with Israelites. They became known as Samaritans.

When the Jewish exiles returned they refused the offer of cooperation from the Samaritans because they regarded them as racially and religiously impure. So began centuries of mutual antagonism.

The Samaritans erected a rival temple on Mt Gerizim in about 400BC. The Jewish Hasmonean ruler, John Hyrcanus, destroyed it in about 108BC.

The Jews would never ask favours of Samaritans for fear of becoming ceremonially unclean. Shortly after the time of Jesus, Samaritan women became officially regarded by Jews as in a state of perpetual ceremonial uncleanness.

To drink from a Samaritan woman's cup would be regarded as especially defiling. The rabbis also regarded talking to a woman, even a Jewish woman, as a waste of time.

The Samaritans only accepted the Pentateuch (the

first five books of the Bible) on the basis of Deuteronomy 34:10 'Since then, no prophet has risen in Israel like Moses, whom the Lord knew face to face.' But they did expect the 'second Moses', the great prophet to come. They called him the *Taheb* which means 'Restorer'.

In the light of all this, it is clear that Jesus showed great respect and love to the Samaritan woman by talking to her and asking her to give him a drink in her own cup. But notice how he deals with her, coming as she did from what was regarded as, to some degree, another faith group:

Look at John 4:
  a. He begins to challenge her immediately about who he is and about eternal life (vv10,14).
  b. He challenges her to repentance (vv16-18).
  c. He ignores her reference to Samaritan tradition (vv12,20-21).
  d. He points out the inadequacy of Samaritan religion, based as it was, only on the Pentateuch. And he makes the 'exclusivist' statement that salvation is from the Jews (v22).
  e. He then finally reveals himself as the Messiah.

Evidently she came to faith in him, as did her fellow townspeople (vv39-42).

So Jesus showed great respect to the woman, but he can hardly be regarded as showing a positive attitude to Samaritan religion. He made 'exclusivist' statements about salvation only being from the Jews and about eternal life being available from him.

(See For Further Study.)

The 'Other Sheep'

In John 10:16 Jesus refers to 'other sheep not of this sheep pen'. Commentators agree that this refers to the

Gentiles. Yet some people argue that they are people of other faiths who come to salvation through those faiths.

However the passage clearly indicates the characteristics of Christ's 'sheep':

1. What do the sheep do?

Jn 10:16

2. Whom do they know?

Jn 10:14

3. How do they have access to salvation?

Jn 10:7-10

Clearly these 'other sheep' have a personal relationship with Christ. The passage therefore cannot be used to support a positive attitude towards other faiths.

Cornelius

Cornelius was a God-fearing Gentile and probably an adherent of the synagogue, but not a proselyte (convert to Judaism). He came to faith in Christ. We shall examine his story in detail in Section 8.

Paul in Athens

1. What was Paul's reaction to the idolatry in Athens?

Acts 17:16

He says the Athenians are very 'religious' (v22). The

original Greek word could also mean 'superstitious'. It certainly was not used as a compliment because speakers to the Areopagus were not allowed to use compliments to gain a hearing (see For Further Study).

2. What did he use to start his sermon?

Acts 17:23

He used it as a point of contact because it was dedicated to any god the Athenians may have left out. It was therefore quite legitimate for Paul to use it as a point of contact for saying they had omitted Yahweh, the one true God! There is no affirmation here of the 'other objects of worship' or idols.

3. Standing beneath the Parthenon (the magnificent temple of Pallas Athene, goddess of wisdom), what does Paul say to the crowd?

Acts 17:24

It is true that Paul quoted their poets (v28). But he also contradicted their respected philosophers, the Epicureans and Stoics (see v18). He stated that God was a personal creator, distinct from creation itself (vv24-25). This contradicted the Stoic pantheism (belief that the universe is god and that god is therefore impersonal).

He also taught that God planned the times and places in which the various nations would live (v26). This contradicted the Epicureans who put everything down to chance.

4. How does Paul describe their idolatry?

Acts 17:29-30

This would be a very unpopular statement because the Athenians prided themselves on their knowledge. He also challenges them to repent.

5. Why does he say they need to repent of their ignorant idolatry?

Acts 17:31

Paul does state in v.30 that 'In the past God *overlooked* their ignorance.' Whereas there is certainly no positive attitude here to pagan Greek religion, there is a hint of mercy. (See Section 8 on the unevangelised.)

[See For Further Study for more on Acts 17.]

Romans 2:14-16
This passage speaks of the Gentiles, who do not have the written law, doing by nature what the law requires. Much has been made of it to support the 'inclusivist' view of people from other faiths unwittingly serving God and so finding salvation. But verse 16 shows clearly that the final judgment will be through Christ.

The passage is, in fact, pointing out that pagans had a moral nature and conscience, even though they didn't have the written law. The whole thrust of Romans is that salvation, for both Jew and Gentile, is not through works but through faith in Christ.

(See the For Further Study section)

What about the salvation of Jews after Christ?

Nicodemus

1. Who was Nicodemus according to the following passages?

Jn 3:1

Jn 3:10

He was a Jewish religious leader. It appears he was a sincere and spiritual man.

2. What did Jesus say to him?

Jn 3:3,5,7

Nicodemus asks how this can happen.

3. What is Jesus reply?

Jn 3:14-15

Jesus is uncompromising: Nicodemus' sincere Jewish faith would not save him (bring him into the kingdom of God). He must be born again through faith in Christ. The relevance of this to our attitude to other faiths, and particularly to evangelism amongst Jewish people, is obvious.

Romans 10:1-3

Paul makes it clear that his fellow-Jews are zealous for God, but their zeal is not based on knowledge. Instead of receiving the righteousness (justification) from God which comes only through faith in Christ, they attempt to establish their own righteousness. This passage shows that this attempt is doomed to failure. In fact much of the Book of Romans argues the point that both Jews and Gentiles can only be saved by faith in Christ, not by keeping the law.

If Jews, with their revelation of Yahweh and their zeal for him are not saved until they come to faith in Christ, what hope is there for people of other faiths? We therefore need to be urgent in evangelism, but we shall consider the matter of those who do not get a chance to hear the gospel in Section 8.

> ### *GROUP DISCUSSION*
>
> Many of those who hold that the Bible is positive towards other faiths actually have misunderstood the nature of Christianity. They think we can have a relationship with God through 'good works' rather than faith. It is therefore a short step to thinking that those of other religions who try to live a good life are accepted by God.
>
> What does the Bible actually say about the relationship between faith and works? (If you need help, turn to the Notes at the end of Section 3).

FOR FURTHER STUDY

THE PLURALISTIC BACKGROUND OF THE NEW TESTAMENT

Harold Netland, *op.cit.*, p11, points out that 'The world of the New Testament was characterized by tremendous social, intellectual, and religious ferment.... Even within Palestine itself, Jews were confronted with alien values, beliefs and practices. The many Jews in the Diaspora...(faced) the formidable challenge presented by Greek philosophy and literature (and they) had to contend with the many popular religious movements of the day—the cults of Asclepius or

Artemis-Diana, the "mystery religions" of Osiris and Isis, Mithras, Adonis, or Eleusis, the ubiquitous cult of the Roman emperor, and the many popularized versions of Stoicism, Cynicism, and Epicureanism...there are striking parallels between the first-century Mediterranean world and that of the West today.'

On pp258f Netland comments on Paul Knitter's contention that the NT writers acquired their exclusivist view of Christianity from the surrounding culture. He writes, 'The first century Mediterranean world was highly relativistic and syncretistic.... If the writers of the New Testament were indeed as influenced by the prevailing assumptions of the surrounding culture as Knitter suggests, one would expect to find in the New Testament not the exclusive statements about Christ one does find, but precisely the opposite.'

THE CANAANITE WOMAN (Mt 15:22ff)

Towards a Theology for Inter-Faith Dialogue, op.cit., p24, says, 'When the woman protests that even children and dogs share the same diet, she shows that Jesus is making a false distinction between Jew and Gentile. Jesus marvellously accepts the argument, and confirms her view. He learns from her, his own boundaries are being enlarged, his attitudes shifted by a woman, a voteless pagan, who for his disciples was just a nuisance.' This offensive piece of special pleading is convincing only to those with a 'low' Christology and is certainly not an interpretation required by the passage.

MATTHEW 25:34-40

Dr R. T. France, *Tyndale NT Commentaries, Matthew* (IVP: Leicester, 1985), p355, comments on Matthew 25:34-40, 'Until fairly recently it was generally assumed that this passage grounded eternal salvation on works of kindness to all in need...and that therefore its message was a sort of humanitarian ethic, with no specifically Christian content. As such, it was an embarrassment to those who based their understanding of the gospel on Paul's teaching that one is justified by faith in Christ and not by "good works". Was Matthew (or Jesus?) then against Paul?

'More recent interpreters have insisted, however, that such an interpretation does not do justice to the description of those in need as Jesus' *brothers*, nor to the use elsewhere in Matthew of language about "these little ones"... It is therefore increasingly accepted that the criterion of judgment is not kindness to the needy in general, but the response of the nations to disciples in need. The passage is sometimes described as an expansion of the theme of 10:40-42, where the gift of a cup of water is specifically "because he is a disciple", so that "he who receives you receives me". Opinions vary as to whether Jesus has in mind specifically Christian *missionaries* (as the context of chap 10 suggests), or pastors and teachers, or some other special group within the number of disciples (those insignificant ones who are "greatest in the kingdom of heaven", 18:3-4). But on any of these views the criterion of judgment becomes not mere philanthropy, but men's response to the kingdom of heaven as it is presented to them in the person of Jesus' "brothers". It is therefore, as in 7:21-23, ultimately a question of their relationship to Jesus himself.'

J. C. Fenton, *Saint Matthew, Pelican NT Commentaries* (Penguin: Harmondsworth, 1963), p402, compares 25:40 with 10:42 and comments, 'Matthew probably thought of the brethren here as the disciples of Jesus; but in the original parable it may have referred to anyone in distress.' (The former confirms France's view and the latter is speculation.)

F. D. Bruner, *Matthew Vol.2, The Churchbook, Matthew 13-28* (Word: Dallas, 1990), pp912ff, points out that what he calls the 'Serving Christians Interpretation' (the interpretation given by France) is supported by Luther, Calvin, Wellhausen, W. C. Allen, W. D. Davies, K. Stendahl, H. B. Green, L. Cope, J. Lambrecht etc.

Bruner himself comments, 'The strength of the Serving Christians Interpretation is its consonance with Matthew 10 and 18, where serving Christians was also the point of Jesus' teaching. The ministry of this interpretation is its encouraging Christians with their importance to Jesus Christ. The theological advantage of this interpretation is protection from a doctrine of salvation by good works (works-righteousness). A doctrine of salvation by good works could seem to make Jesus Christ and faith in him dispensable for most of the world. Hence Reformation and Evangelical theologies often have an understandable affinity for an interpretation of Matthew 25 that protects our text from teaching misleading doctrine.'

Bruner, however, thinks that 'both interpretations are true, sequentially. Historically, Jesus may have given this teaching with "Christian"...intentions first of all and later the church universalized his teaching in the ethical direction of the poor...'

He believes that many will unconsciously receive Christ in others. But they will not be saved because of their love, but because of the death of Christ. He adds (p925), 'No human love is ever sufficiently loving to deserve God. A much greater price than the love of fallen human beings must be paid to earn the holy God. That price has been paid by the blood of Jesus Christ exclusively. But now, in amazing magnanimity, *this very Christ* swings heaven's door wide to let in simple care-givers.' He asks, 'What will happen to those who have not heard the gospel?' Answer: 'They will be judged by whether they receive Christ or not *in others*.'

This is a clear exposition of the Inclusivist view. Although popular, it suffers from a lack of biblical justification. We have seen that Matthew 25 is, to say the least, open to different interpretations and so an inadequate basis for Inclusivism.

Bruner gives four reasons for preferring what he calls the 'Serving the Needy Interpretation' (ie 'brothers' = all the needy, not just disciples):

a. The finality and universality of the text (last judgment, all nations).

b. The surprise of the righteous as opposed to the intentional service of Christians in 10:40-42;

c. The four lists of the needy which define 'the least'.

d. The wider context of the four warning stories referring to the seriousness of the judgment of God for Christians.

It seems to us that these four points are inconclusive. (a), (c) and (d) could as easily support the 'Serving Christians

Interpretation' and (b) is overstated since even Christians very often do not consciously think they are serving Christ when they serve one another.

It is important to add that Bruner also says, 'Many never become sufficiently unselfish (I think Paul would say "*none* become sufficiently unselfish") and so will perish unless they explicitly meet the living Christ who transforms human nature. Hence the gospel of Jesus' salvation by faith must always be preached, for true lovers of others are rare. But some do become such lovers, Jesus here teaches, unconscious of, yet mysteriously in touch with, *him*—in the person of the needy other...' (p921).

A. W. Argyle, *The Gospel According to Matthew, Cambridge Bible Commentary* (CUP: London, 1963), p193, comments on Matthew 25:35-36, 'Service to Christ's disciples is service to Christ himself.'

E. M. B. Green, *Matthew for Today* (Hodder & Stoughton: London, 1988), p243, comments on the passage, 'people who have never heard the good news...will be judged by their response to what light they had, in particular by their response to the "brethren" of Jesus, whether these be his Jewish or Christian brethren.'

Like Bruner, we see no contradiction between justification by faith and a final judgment by works. Faith without works is dead. A 'believer' with few or no good works is no believer. But that is a very different thing from saying that those who do good works without believing in Christ will be saved on that day. R. T. France is surely right in his interpretation that the passage is about a response to Jesus as seen in his disciples.

JOHN 4

The Church of England report, *Multi-Faith Worship?* (Church House Publishing: London, 1992), para 47 says, 'As the story of Jesus' encounter with the Samaritan woman (John 4) makes clear, although the Judaeo-Christian tradition of worship has a special place in God's purposes, it, together with other traditions which "worship what they do not know", will be transcended and fulfilled in Christ.'

It is true that Judaeo-Christian worship is imperfect. But the implication of this statement appears to be that non-Christian is merely less special than Christian worship. John 4 will not bear such a conclusion:

i. Samaritan worship was based on the Pentateuch: most non-Christian religions do not have such a biblical base.

ii. Jesus says the Samaritans worship what they do not know because they have not accepted the fuller revelation of God in the rest of the Hebrew Scriptures (v22).

iii. He stresses that the chosen people do know God and that salvation comes from them (v22). He challenges her to believe in him (vv10,13-14).

It is therefore not legitimate to infer from this specific context that the worship of other religions is merely less special or less acceptable than Christian worship. Jesus makes it quite clear in this passage that salvation and eternal life are available only through faith in him.

ACTS 17

Professor F. F. Bruce, *Commentary on the Book of Acts*, English Text (Eerdmans: Grand Rapids, 1956), p355, comments on the word 'religious' (or 'superstitious') in v22. Quoting Lucian, *Anacharsis 19*, he says, 'In any case, Paul is stating a fact, not paying a compliment; we are told that it was forbidden to use complimentary exordia when addressing the Areopagus, in hope of securing good will.'

Commenting (p356) on the phrase 'To an Unknown God', (v23), he states, 'This God whom they worshipped, while confessing that they did not know him, was the God whom he now proposed to make known to them. Only he did not express himself quite so personally as if unreservedly identifying the 'unknown god' of the inscription with the God he proclaimed; rather he announced that since they acknowledged their ignorance of the divine nature, he would tell them the truth about it...their ignorance rather than their worship is thus underscored, and Paul is indicating that he will inform them with regard to that which they acknowledge ignorance.'

Professor Bruce adds (p360), 'Paul is here dealing with the

responsibility of all men as God's creatures to give Him the honour which is His due. And this honour is certainly not given if men envisage the divine nature in terms of plastic images... Even if pagan philosophers rationalise the images as mere symbols of the invisible divinity, the great bulk of the worshippers pay divine homage to the images themselves.'

ROMANS 2:14-16

Professor J. R. Edwards, *New International Biblical Commentary, Romans* (Hendrickson, Peabody: Massachusetts, 1992), pp70-72, comments on v14, 'Here and in verse 15, where Paul speaks of the law written on Gentile hearts, he argues that even people without religious instruction are responsible moral agents. Cranfield understands Gentiles here to mean Christian Gentiles, but that is surely reading too much into the verse... Paul has not yet introduced Jesus Christ into the discussion of Jews and Gentiles (with the exception of 1:16-17). His whole argument depends on the premise that apart from Christ Jews and Gentiles are deserving of God's wrath. Paul is contending for an innate moral sense in humanity, to whose voice Gentiles are as bound as are Jews to the Torah. In so arguing he is in good company, not only with the Jewish tradition but also with the pagan...'

'Not uncommonly Romans 2:12-14 is cited as evidence that there is salvation apart from Jesus Christ. This passage does not answer the question in the affirmative. Verse 16 explicitly says that Jesus Christ will be the standard of judgment for all peoples... The point of this verse is not that Gentiles can be saved by an inner law, but that both Jews and Gentiles have failed to live up to the laws which they have respectively received, and that both are justly condemned. The standards will be different for each, but the verdict will be the same for both.'

Professor F. F. Bruce, *Romans, Tyndale NT Commentary* (IVP: Leicester, 1989), p86, comments, 'Paul and his readers knew pagans who led upright lives in accordance with the dictates of conscience (although this was not the ground of their justification before God)...'

'K. Barth holds that Gentile Christians are in view here (similarly Cranfield...) but this scarcely suits the context.'

Professor Douglas Moo, *The Wycliffe Exegetical Commentary* (Moody: Chicago, 1991), holds that it is non-Christian Gentiles being referred to and he comments, p150, 'Some have seized on the reference to "excusing" [v15] as evidence that this final verdict could bring salvation to some Gentiles apart from the gospel. But this misses the connection in which the idea stands. Bengel is on the mark: "The concessive participle, even, shows that the thoughts have far more to accuse, than defend, and the defense itself... does not extend to the whole, but only to a part of the conduct, and this very part in turn proves us to be debtors to the whole, 1:20" '

C. E. B. Cranfield, *International Critical Commentary, The Epistle to the Romans* (T & T Clark: Edinburgh, 1975), as we have seen, interprets these verses as referring to Christian Gentiles. But he comments on v13 as follows, 'In its context in Romans this sentence can hardly be intended to imply that there are some who are doers of the law in the sense that they so fulfil it as to earn God's justification' (p155). Commenting on verses 14-16 he makes it clear that a salvation by works interpretation is incompatible with 3:9, 20, 23 (p156).

CHAPTER 7
WHAT ABOUT IDOLATRY?

This subject is very important today as there is a revival of interest in and sympathy for ancient tribal or other religions which involve idolatry. There are therefore many attempts to justify idolatry.

It is important to understand that there are various different approaches to the use of images in religion. Not all are idolatrous. Roger Hooker (see For Further Study section) has described them as follows:

a. 'The Whitewashers'

These people reject all images. They are the strictest group which includes Jews, Muslims, some Protestant groups, early Buddhists, Sikhs and some Hindus.

b. 'The Symbolists'

These people use pictures, statues, crosses, crucifixes or other images but do not believe that in any sense the deity or some semi-divine being dwells within them.

An example is that one view of Communion (associated with the reformer Zwingli) is mere symbolism. A slightly more advanced symbolist view of Communion, associated with John Calvin is that by taking the bread and wine (which remain merely bread and wine) in faith we really do feed spiritually on Christ. But there is no divine presence in the elements.

c. 'The Incense-Burners'

This group believe that some divine figure or one closely associated with the divinity is in some way present within the idol. Many Hindus would belong to this group. But some Christians would too, with respect to communion or a superstitious view of statues of Mary.

d. 'The Literalists'

This is the crudest form of idolatry. These people believe the deity is totally contained in the image.

It is only the 'incense-burners' and 'literalists' which concern us in this session.

The Old Testament attitude to idolatry

A total ban on idols/images

1. What does Exodus say about idols?

Ex 20:4-6

2. What does Leviticus say about sacred carved stones?

Lev 26:1

3. What does Deuteronomy say about those carving or casting an image?

Deut 27:15

4. What reason does Deuteronomy give against idolatry?

Deut 4:15-18

5. What does Deuteronomy forbid?

Deut 4:19

A total ban on associating the Divine Presence with images

The Bible does not merely condemn the 'literalists' who believe the deity is totally contained in the image but also the 'incense-burners' who believe the deity is in some way present within the image. The sacred stones condemned in Leviticus 26:1 were understood in an 'incense-burner' way. The same can be said about the golden calves of Exodus 32:4; Deuteronomy 9:12,16 and 1 Kings 12:28-31.

The point can also be made that it is hard to know where the 'incense-burner' approach stops and the 'literalist' approach begins. Also, although the founders of religions and some leaders may only regard an idol as something to help a person worship God, the majority often worship the idol itself.

A scathing condemnation of idols

1. How are idols described in the following passages:

Deut 29:17

1 Sam 12:21

1 Kings 16:13,26

Is 41:29

Jer 3:24

Jer 10:5

Jer 16:18

Jer 32:34

2. Read Isaiah's biting sarcasm about idols in Isaiah 44:9-20. What does he see idolaters as bowing down to?

Is 44:19

Idols are 'worthless, the objects of mockery' (Jer 51:18). Isaiah calls them *elilim*, a pun on *elohim* ('gods'). *Elilim* means 'nonentities' (Is 2:8,18-20; Hab 2:18). On 38 occasions Ezekiel uses a word of idols which means 'dung pellets' (eg Ezek 6:4-14). Habakkuk describes them using a word meaning 'godlets' (Hab 2:18).

Isaiah calls the main god of the Ammonites Molech. The real name is probably Melech (King) but Isaiah has inserted the vowels from *bosheth* (shame). Similarly *Baal-zebub* (or *Beelzebub*) 'lord of the flies' may have been Hebrew mockery for *Baal-zebul* 'lord of the high places'. Yahweh judges the 'gods' of the nations (Ex 12:12; Num 33:4). For example, it is likely that the plagues in Egypt were directed at her gods, eg the Nile god *Hopi* (Ex 7:19), the frog or toad goddess *Heqt* (Ex 8:2) and the Sun god *Ra* or *Re* (Ex 10:21).

3. What did the Lord command the Israelites to do in the following passages?

Deut 7:5,25

Deut 12:2-3

Deut 17:2-5

Deut 18:10-12

4. Read 2 Kings 23:4-25
(See also 1 Kings 18:40; 2 Chron 23:17)

It is true, of course, that much ancient idolatry was

associated with depraved and barbaric practices. A great deal of the worship was linked with fertility rites and led to sacred prostitution and other sexual debauchery. The Asherah was a sacred tree or wooden pole symbolising the Canaanite goddess of the same name. She was goddess of the sea, consort to the high god El and linked with Baal too. Asherah was mother of the gods. Asherah poles were erected adjacent to many altars in Israel and were roundly condemned by the prophets.

Then there was Ashtoreth, goddess of fertility, love and war (1 Kings 11:5). She is also known as Astarte or Ishtar 'the Queen of Heaven' (Jer 7:18; 44:25). Clay plaques depicting naked female images with exaggerated sexual organs have been discovered in Israel.

Commenting on Isaiah 57:8, Westermann[1] says, 'the symbol behind the door' (condemned by the prophet) 'probably refers to the representation of the phallus as a symbol of fertility', (*op.cit.*, p324). J. B. Taylor[2] points out that the stone pillar often associated with Canaanite altars 'may well have been regarded as a phallic symbol'.

Then there was the terrible practice of child sacrifice (2 Kings 17:31; 23:10; Jer 32:35). Jeremiah refers to Topheth which is a place of child sacrifice and may also mean 'fireplace' (7:31f). Apparently children were thrown into the fire pit there.

Although ancient idolatry was associated with gross immorality and human sacrifice, it seems clear from the OT material that idolatry was condemned per se, not just because of these factors.

There is much idealising in the post-Christian West of both ancient religions and modern tribal or idolatrous religions. It should be remembered that these religions in some cases include debased practices and very often hold their adherents in the grip of fear.

(For further material on the OT attitude to idolatry see For Further Study section.)

The New Testament attitude to idolatry

Idolatry is condemned

1. How is idolatry described in the following passages?

1 Pet 4:3

Gal 5:19-20

2. What can idolatry lead to?

Rom 1:21-32

3. What will happen to idolaters according to the following passages?

1 Cor 6:9

Gal 5:19-21

Rev 22:14-15

Rev 21:8

4. How should believers respond to idolatry according to the following passages?

1 Cor 10:14

1 Jn 5:21

5. How does Paul react to idolatry in Athens?

Acts 17:16

It may be argued that Paul is here only condemning a 'literalist' approach to idolatry. But this is by no means certain and in view of the OT condemnation of 'incense-burning' it is unconvincing to argue that the NT only condemns 'literalist' idolatry.

In Athens (as we saw in the previous Section) Paul was greatly distressed at the widespread idolatry (Acts 17:16). He said the Athenians are very 'religious' (v22), which, as we have already seen, could mean 'superstitious'. He focused on their ignorance rather than their worship.

Standing beneath the Parthenon, he proclaimed that God does not dwell in temples or need anything from men. He contradicted their Stoic pantheism and Epicurean philosophy of chance (vv24-26), and called their idolatry ignorance to be repented of (v30). It is not legitimate to say (as some are doing today) that Paul commended their religion.

6. What did Paul say about idols in Ephesus?

Acts 19:26

In Ephesus Paul confronted the cult of the goddess Artemis and caused a riot. Artemis (also called Diana or Cybele) was the mother goddess of fertility who was worshipped in many parts of the then-known world. Her image in the temple at Ephesus (one of the seven wonders of the world) was believed to have fallen from heaven. It may have been a meteorite which bore an image resembling a many-breasted female. Her worship involved sacred prostitution.

Idolatry is demonic

1. What are idols according to the following passages?

1 Cor 8:4

Gal 4:8

2. What does Paul say about the nature of idolatry?

1 Cor 10:20

Idols are not real gods (1 Cor 8:4-6; Gal 4:8 cf 1 Cor 12:2; 1 Thess 1:9). In fact 'the sacrifices of pagans are offered to demons' (1 Cor 10:20). This is a very serious reason for avoiding all idolatry—because it has an evil, demonic dimension.

The early church in the first council (at Jerusalem) made a resolution that Gentiles who had become Christians should abstain from food polluted by idols (Acts 15:19). But this left some questions in the mind of the church in Corinth, which Paul addresses. He deals with two questions about idolatry in 1 Corinthians 8 and 10. First, whether Christians should eat meat bought from the market which may well have been offered to idols. Secondly, whether Christians should participate, when invited, in idol feasts in temples.

i. Paul clearly states that idols are nothing, they are not real gods (8:4; 10:19). Therefore to eat meat bought in the market which may have been offered to idols is of no consequence in itself (8:8). However, some Christians with more sensitive consciences are not yet convinced that idols are unreal. If they eat such meat they will defile their consciences (8:7). It is therefore wrong for those with less sensitive consciences, who regard idols and their sacrifices as nothing, to eat such meat if it is a stumbling block to the person with the more sensitive conscience (8:9-13; 10:23-24).

The Christian is free to eat meat bought in the market which may have been offered to an idol, without asking questions (10:25-26). Similarly, he may eat meat in the home of a pagan friend which has the same origin (10:27). But if anyone says the meat has been offered to idols, then the Christian should not eat it for the sake of the other person's conscience. Whether the latter is a believer or not, he may gain the impression that the Christian approves of idolatry (10:25-32).

ii. A Christian should, however, never be involved in an idol feast in a pagan temple (10:21). The sacrifices of pagans are offered to demons, so participation in idolatry is participation in demon worship. Those who visit the temple and eat that portion of the meat offered to idols which is for worshippers to share are 'participants with demons.' This is totally incompatible with participation in Communion (10:14-22 cf Acts 15:20, 29; 21:25).

In summary, it is wrong to take part in idolatrous worship and feasting, but meat which may have been offered to idols and is bought in the market place cannot contaminate a Christian.

CONCLUSION

Idolatry is wrong because:

(1) It breaks the law of God (which we have seen excludes 'incense-burning' as well as 'literalism'—Ex 20:4-6; Lev 26:1; Deut 4:15-19).

(2) It does not give honour to God (Rom 1:21-25) who cannot be represented by a mere idol or contained within physical temples (Acts 17:24). The idea that mere men can be deified (made into gods), which is at the heart of much modern idolatry or New Age teaching, also degrades the idea of divinity.

(3) It has a demonic dimension (1 Cor 10:20).

(4) It is fundamentally selfish. William Barclay[3] comments, 'The root sin of idolatry is that it is selfish. A man makes an idol. He brings it offerings and addresses prayers to it. Why? So that his own schemes and dreams may be furthered. His worship is for his own sake and not for God's.' This is widely true of modern idolatry.

(5) It involves at least a danger of 'literalism'.

(6) It involves a danger of immorality (Rom 1:21ff).

From the biblical material it is clear that both forms of idolatry ('incense-burning' and 'literalism') are ruled out. The belief that some divine figure or one closely related to divinity is in some way present within the idol as well as the belief that the deity is totally contained in the image are both contrary to Scripture. It is more likely that idol-worshippers are in touch with demons. Christians should not be involved with or appear to agree to the practices of such beliefs. Jesus is the image of the invisible God (Col 1:15) and in him all the fullness of the Deity lives in bodily form (Col 2:9). What need do we have of mere idols?

GROUP DISCUSSION

Either a. It is possible for any one of us to give to another person, thing, idea or image more importance than God. Discuss how some Christians may be in danger of idolatrous attitudes.

Or b. How can Paul's answers to the questions about idolatrous worship and meat offered to idols (1 Cor 8 & 10) be applied in a modern multicultural situation?

Notes

1. Isaiah 40–66, OT Library (SCM: London, 1969), p.324.

2. *Ezekiel, Tyndale OT Commentaries* (IVP: Leicester, 1969), p90.

3. *The Letter to the Romans, Daily Study Bible* (St. Andrews Press: Edinburgh, 1975), p28.

FOR FURTHER STUDY

HOOKER ON IDOLATRY

Roger Hooker, *What is Idolatry?*, CRPOF (British Council of Churches: London, 1986), writes that 'incense-burners' and 'literalists' tend to have close ties with the land and stress the feminine aspects of divinity (goddesses). This may be linked with the fertility of the soil (p9). He also points out that many Hindus feel they cannot worship without images (pp12-13).

The booklet states that in 600 AD Pope Gregory the Great defended the 'Symbolist' position so, by implication, repudiating the 'whitewashing' norm of the OT (p38). Then John of Damascus taught that since Jesus was a man and images of men were allowable, images of Jesus were allowable. He went further and said that since God's power in Scripture could work through Elisha's staff and bones, Peter's shadow, Paul's handkerchief, etc., he could also work in power through images. The Second Council of Nicea accepted this view, which became the official position of the Roman Catholic and Orthodox churches (pp39-42).

Hooker suggests that, as John of Damascus argued, the Incarnation modified the OT ban on images. God revealed himself as a man and it is permissible to make images of men. He argues that this could justify an 'incense-burning' approach like that of the Second Nicene Council (p46).

Most people concerned with a positive approach to other faiths would be unhappy with the 'literalist' or crude form of idolatry. But Hooker and many others try to justify the view that the divinity is associated with the idol and so we can worship God through the idol. (This is the incense-burner approach). We shall take issue with this view and seek to give further evidence that the 'incense-burner' approach to images is condemned in Scripture.

THE OLD TESTAMENT ON IDOLATRY

It is important to note that the OT condemns the 'incense-burner' attitude to idols as well as the 'literalist' approach, as the following quotations from commentators indicate.

Commenting on Leviticus 26:1, R. K.Harrison, *Leviticus, Tyndale OT Commentaries* (IVP: Leicester, 1980), p231, describes a graven image as a 'cultic representation of deity'; the pillar or stone as a 'tangible indication of the presence of El or Baal.' Similarly John Gray, *I & II Kings* (SCM OT Library: London, 1964), p311, commenting on 1 Kings 14:23, writes, 'The standing stones (*massebot*) as a feature of these sanctuaries were symbols of the presence of the deity or memorials of the reception of a theophany.' The NIV comments on Isaiah 44:17, 'Whereas those who worshipped idols associated the god with the idol, for Isaiah there was no god for the idol to represent, so he depicts idolatry as worship of a mere "block of wood" (v19)'.

Hooker includes an important quotation from Gerhard von Rad, *Old Testament Theology, Vol 1* (Oliver and Boyd: 1970), p214, quoted in R. Hooker, *op.cit.*, pp30-31), 'The pagan religions knew as well as Israel did that deity is invisible, that it transcends all human ability to comprehend it, and that it cannot be captured or compromised in a material object. But this did not deter them from consecrating cultic images to it...the image is first and foremost the bearer of revelation...As against this idea, the veto on images in the OT is by no means a general religious truth, but the most abrupt affront to this concept of deity.' This quotation from von Rad therefore substantiates the view of an OT veto against the 'incense burner' position.

Professor P. C. Craigie, *The Book of Deuteronomy* (Eerdmans: Grand Rapids, 1976), p136), writes, 'The more sophisticated Egyptian and Canaanites no doubt understood that

WHAT ABOUT IDOLATRY? 109

their physical images were not in themselves divine, but only representations of divinity.'

The prohibitions on idolatry include making images of Yahweh. By definition such an idol would be a means through which Yahweh would be worshipped. It would not (except in a very debased form of Yahwism) be regarded as Yahweh himself. But both approaches are condemned as idolatry. Hooker's distinction between these two approaches is not new, but is found in the ancient world. To worship God through an image and not the image itself is still idolatry, according to Scripture. In any case, as Hooker admits, 'It is not always possible to say where the incense burning stops and the literalism begins.' (*op.cit.*, p.24).

The condemnation of the golden calf incidents is illuminating here (Ex 32:4; Deut 9:12,16; 1 Kings 12:28-31). J. A. Thompson, *Deuteronomy, Tyndale OT Commentaries* (IVP: Leicester, 1974), p141, comments, 'It has been suggested that this image is to be compared with images of beasts in other Near Eastern religions which acted as supporting pedestals for deities. Several excellent examples are extant today. In particular the storm god of Canaan stood on the back of a bull. Other deities stood on other animals. The animal was not intended as an object of worship but as a symbol of the deity. In some examples in the ancient Near East animals appear alone, but the context suggests that they symbolise a deity. The attempt to symbolise Yahweh's presence among his people by a golden calf could only lead to deep confusion, for it suggested idolatry even if the intention was to give encouragement to the faint-hearted in Israel by symbolising Yahweh's presence among them.'

Similarly Gray, commenting on 1 Kings 12:28, states: 'The golden calves, misrepresented by orthodox Jewish opinion as idols, were rather the places where the presence of Yahweh was visualised, like the ark in the Temple in Jerusalem and the bull pedestals of Baal-Hadad in Syrian sculpture as pointed out by Albright.' (*op.cit.*, p.290).

A. E. Cundall, *Judges, Tyndale OT Commentaries* (IVP: Leicester, 1968), p184, makes a similar point in connection with Micah's idols in Judges 17. 'It has been suggested that the image may have been in the form of a bull, which is found throughout a wide area in the ancient world as the representation of the deity. The gods were often depicted as standing, or more rarely sitting, on the back of a bull, which by its strength and power of fertility well represented the essence of the nature cults. Aaron made a bull or calf image while Moses was in the holy mountain (Ex 32:4) and, at a later date, Jereboam ben Nebat made similar images to set up at the shrines at Dan and Bethel (1 Kings 12:28-30). Most scholars accept that these were not intended to represent Yahweh but rather to serve as the visible throne upon which the invisible Yahweh was conceived to sit. But the great danger of associating the worship of Yahweh with the bull, the symbol of the Canaanite fertility cults, will be apparent.'

The supreme Canaanite deity, El, was often called the Bull. Baal, his son, could transform himself into a bull, according to the Ras Shamra texts.

The condemnation of the gold calf images may have been partly because of the bull's association with pagan religion, especially as the cherubim were seen as providing a visible pedestal for the invisible throne of Yahweh (1 Sam 4:4; 2 Sam 6:2; 2 Kings 19:15; 1 Chron 13:6; Ps 80:1; 99:1; Is 37:16). But 'they were not objects of worship so much as symbols of the angelic beings serving God, rather like the Temple guardians of the Assyrian temple.' (A. Cole, *Exodus, Tyndale OT Commentaries* [IVP: Leicester, 1973], p155.)

The ban on the calf or bull pedestal shows how strictly the OT sought to rule out idolatry. With the exception of the Cherubim, on the ark, even images indirectly representing the presence of Yahweh were ruled out.

It is clear then that the Canaanites etc, distinguished between the cultic objects and the gods themselves. In any case, logically it is difficult to see how a thorough-going 'literalist' approach could be held other than within the most debased form of polytheism. How could Baal worshippers, for example, who saw Baal as a wider than local god, think of him as 'totally contained within the image: the image literally (being) the deity, and vice versa.' (R. Hooker, *op.cit.*, p9)? It seems to us that they must have been 'incense-burners'.

However, the connection between god and image was intimate. 'Once these cult symbols were destroyed, the

Canaanites could not make contact with the gods and in course of time these would be forgotten and their name would disappear from the place where they had been worshipped.' (J. A. Thompson, *op.cit.*, p165). This relates to Hooker's quotation of a devotee of Rama and a Buddhist who regarded images as essential to worship (R. Hooker, *op.cit.*, pp12-13).

C.Westermann, *Isaiah 40-66* (SCM OT Library: London, 1969), pp179ff, commenting on the downfall of Babylon and her gods in Isaiah 46:1-4 says, 'What does it mean for a god to be bound up with his image? This is only revealed now, at the moment when disaster is engulfing a country. Then in the hour of disaster, it is suddenly made plain that, even if the god is not identical with his image, he is connected with it beyond hope of separation. Where the only possibility is flight, the statue is not mere symbol: the fugitives must take it along with them. This tells its own story. It means the sudden, fantastic reversal of roles. The worshippers are obliged to save their gods, for the gods cannot save themselves. Instead of the gods bearing their people at a time when ruin threatens to engulf the latter, they themselves require to be borne, they become a burden.'

It is safe to conclude that the OT strongly condemns not only the 'literalist' but also the 'incense-burner' approach to idols. There is a total ban on associating the divine presence with images.

DEUTERONOMY 4:19; 29:26

But is this contradicted in Deuteronomy 4:19 'And when you look up to the sky and see the sun, the moon and the stars—all the heavenly array—do not be enticed into bowing down to them and worshipping things the Lord your God has apportioned to all the nations under heaven.' Also Deuteronomy 29:26 'They went off and worshipped other gods and bowed down to them, gods they did not know, gods he had not given them.'?

These verses are made much of by those looking for a positive attitude to other religions, although Deuteronomy 4:19 could be taken simply as meaning that the Lord has created heavenly bodies for the benefit of all. And Deuteronomy 29:26 is stating that God has *not* given gods to anyone. However we shall examine the commentaries in more depth.

The Anglican Report, *Multi-Faith Worship?*, para.49, says, 'Even in Deuteronomy, which contains texts which strongly deny the existence of other gods, there are hints that these "gods" have been given to the Gentile nations by the true God—see, for example, Deuteronomy 4:19; 29:26. Provided that the worship of such "gods" was not brought into competition with mainstream Israelite worship, we can see how it had a place in God's purposes and was in a real if limited sense directed to him.'

Professor S. R. Driver, *International Critical Commentary, Deuteronomy* (T & T Clark: Edinburgh, 1902), pp70ff, commenting on Deuteronomy 4:19, says, 'The God of Israel is supreme: He assigns to every nation its objects of worship; and the veneration of the heavenly bodies by the nations (other than Israel) forms part of his providential order of the world. Natural religion, though it may become depraved (Rom 1:21ff), is a witness to some of the deepest needs and instincts of humanity: in default of a purer and higher faith, the yearnings of mankind after a power higher than themselves find legitimate satisfaction in it. Clement of Alexandria... even views the worship of the heavenly bodies as granted to the nations... and as the appointed means of enabling them to rise to something better.'

Professor Gerhard von Rad, *Deuteronomy—A Commentary* (SCM: London, 1966), p50, comments, 'There is a remarkable contrast between the uncompromising enforcement of the prohibition of idols for Israel and the tolerance towards the worship of idols by other nations. Nowhere else in the Old Testament is the idea that Yahweh himself allotted the stars to the nations for their worship (v19) expressed with such broad-mindedness... The explanation that Israel was condemned to be scattered because its worship of idols occurs also in the Deuteronomistic historical writings...'

Professor P. C. Craigie, *The Book of Deuteronomy* (Eerdmans: Grand Rapids, 1976), p137, says, 'These false forms of worship, though assigned by God to other nations (v19) would be antithetic to the revelation of Israel's true religion.'

J. Ridderbos, *Bible Students Commentary—Deuteronomy*, transl. Ed M van der Maas (Regency/Zondervan: Grand Rapids, 1984), p87, comments, 'Even though idolatry is a transgression of God's will and command, it (like all sin) occurs in accordance with his plan and providential governance—"He let all nations go their own way" (Acts 14:16).'

A Jewish scholar, Professor J. Reider, *Deuteronomy* (Jewish Publication Society of America: Philadelphia, 1937), pp52-53, comments on Deuteronomy 4:19, 'According to the Talmud (*Meg.9b*) the Alexandrian translators of the Scriptures found this passage objectionable, since it seems to imply that God permitted all the other nations to worship the celestial bodies; consequently they are said to have added the phrase "to give light to them" (which, however, is wanting in the current Septuagint, but comp. *in ministerium* of the Vulgate). On the other hand, Rab (in *Ab.Zarah 55a*), RSbM and others, are inclined to take the phrase as it stands and to explain it somewhat as follows: God, as the supreme ruler of the universe, assigns to every nation its cult, and while he granted to the Hebrews monotheism, the highest form of worship, he allotted to the heathens the astral cult, which, though inferior, is better than utter ignorance of God and his creation.'

BUT the idea of Yahweh apportioning 'gods' to other nations must be seen in context:

1. As we see in this Section idols and other gods are condemned in the strongest terms. Clearly idolatry and the worship of other gods is totally contrary to the will of Yahweh.

2. However, as Acts 14:15-16 says, Yahweh in the past 'let all the nations go their own way' over idolatry. Everett Harrison, *Acts: The Expanding Church* (Moody: Chicago, 1975), comments (p223), 'God had permitted the nations to go their own way, neither revealing Himself as He did to Israel nor bringing severe judgment on them for their idolatrous practices. But this time of leniency had now passed (cf 17:30-31). And during past generations God had not really been indifferent, but had borne "witness" to Himself as Benefactor of the race by making nature fruitful for the good of man.

However, this is not the same thing as saying that the witness had been understood and received.'

Now the full revelation had come to the Gentiles and so God commanded them to repent of idolatry. 'In the past God overlooked such ignorance (idolatry), but now he commands all people everywhere to repent. For he has set a day when he will judge the world with justice, by the man he has appointed. He has given proof of this to all men by raising him from the dead' (Acts 17:30). It is therefore not true to Scripture to argue that God is in any way positive towards idolatry or the worship of other gods.

3. We do not believe that Deuteronomy 4:19 and 29:26 teach that God apportions gods to the nations. If they did, then the explanation would be as follows. The OT would not describe God as *permitting* idolatry but (typically omitting secondary causes) would be saying that God apportions gods to the nations. One may parallel this with a passage like Isaiah 63:17 which states that Yahweh makes his people wander from him and hardens their hearts so that they do not revere him. Today, we would say that God in his sovereignty allowed his people to wander from him and harden their hearts. Similarly, if the passages were to be interpreted as God apportioning gods, we would say that God in his sovereignty allowed the nations to worship the gods they had chosen.

IDOLATRY AND IMMORALITY

The danger of immorality being associated with idolatry can be facilitated through the fact, as Hooker records, that 'incense-burners and literalists usually do have close ties with the land...They often give an important place to the feminine aspect of divinity, for this is related to the fertility of the soil...' (*op.cit.*, p9). Also, as Hooker points out, in South India, Shiva is approached through the lingam, an image of the male organ (p15). He points out that the lingam is always set in the representation of the female vulva and he seeks to justify this ('purity and impurity are in the eye of the beholder') and to make the astonishing (and offensive) statement that 'The "pillar of fire" referred to in the Bible and other religious books is one form of the same lingam.' (pp18-19). We are not, of course, saying that all involved in goddess worship etc are involved in sexual immorality, but merely that history proves such worship has encouraged immorality.

CHAPTER 8
WHAT ABOUT THE UNEVANGELISED?

We saw in Section 2 how loving, compassionate and merciful God is and that he is perfectly just. Because of this we are bound to ask how he deals (concerning salvation) with those who have never heard the gospel. Are they automatically condemned because they have never heard the message and therefore have never had the opportunity to respond to it? Would this be just? These questions loom large for Christians who believe that, according to Scripture, salvation is only through Christ and faith in him is required. We need to enquire further into what Scripture teaches.

Eternal life is knowing God the Father and Jesus Christ

1. How does Jesus define eternal life?

Jn 17:3

2. Who knows Christ?

Jn 10:14

3. How does a person come to know God?

Jn 14:6-9

118   JESUS THE ONLY SAVIOUR

4. What are some evidences that a person knows God according to the following passages?

1 Jn 2:3-4

1 Jn 4:6

1 Jn 4:7-8

Unbelievers do not know God

1. What was the state of the Ephesians before they trusted in Christ?

Eph 2:12

(For more on Eph 2:12 see For Further Study section.)

'Without God' in the Greek is *atheos* from which we get our word 'atheist'. It is not that they didn't believe in God. They did believe in a god or gods. But they did not have the true and only God—Yahweh. They did not know him.

2. What is said about 'the heathen'?

1 Thess 4:5

3. What is said about 'the world'?

1 Cor 1:21

1 Jn 3:1

Paul writes that there are many 'so-called gods' (1 Cor 8:5) who are not gods (Gal 4:8). But Christian believers know God (Gal 4:9).

4. What does Jesus say about the Jews who reject him?

Jn 8:19

(See also Jn 7:28; 8:55; 15:21; 16:3)

5. What is true of those who reject Christ according to the following passages?

1 Jn 2:22-23

1 Jn 5:12

2 Jn 9

6. What is said about false teachers?

Tit 1:16

Those who reject Christ do not know God or 'have' God. They do not have eternal life which Jesus defined in John 17:3 as knowing the Father and the Son. The fact that these passages state that Jewish people (God's covenant people of old) who reject Christ do not 'have' or know God shows how exclusive the New Testament is. If this is true of the chosen people how much more is it true of those of other faiths?

There are also many who claim to be Christian who do not have a personal relationship with Christ, but are relying on a good life or church attendance for salvation, rather than trusting in what God has done to save us through Jesus Christ.

7. What is the eternal destiny of those who do not know God?

2 Thess 1:6-10

8. How does Paul describe those who are perishing in the following passages?

2 Thess 2:10

2 Thess 2:12

Note that in 2 Thessalonians 1:8 he refers to them as 'those who do not know God and *do not obey* the gospel of our Lord Jesus.' Some of those he has in mind are persecuting believers (2 Thess 1:5-8).

Paul seems to be saying here that those who will be condemned are those who *refuse* to believe the gospel, ie. they hear it but reject it. He does not seem to be referring to those who have never heard the gospel.

General revelation makes it inexcusable not to know about God

1. What does Paul say about God's revelation of himself?

Rom 1:20

Millard Erickson, an evangelical Baptist theologian, believes that the essential elements of the gospel can be known through general revelation. He lists them as follows:

i. The belief in one good powerful God.

ii. The belief that he (man) owes this God perfect obedience to his law.

iii. The consciousness that he does not meet this standard, and therefore is guilty and condemned.

iv. The realization that nothing he can offer God can compensate him (or atone) for this sin and guilt.

v. The belief that God is merciful, and will forgive and accept those who cast themselves upon his mercy.[1]

However, this seems to be only preparation for the gospel, since it omits Jesus and the cross.

2. How does Paul describe those against whom God's wrath is revealed according to the following passages?

Rom 1:18

Rom 1:21

Rom 1:25

Rom 1:28

Clearly Paul is speaking of those who deliberately reject the true revelation of God through creation in favour of idolatry. But we must consider those who have never heard the gospel.

Knowing the Father requires revelation by Christ

What does Jesus say about knowing the Father?

Mt 11:27

It is clear from Romans 1:21 that human beings have some knowledge of God through creation. The Jews to whom Jesus was speaking had further knowledge of God through the Old Testament. But Jesus' knowledge of the Father far surpassed all this. It is only those who come to know Christ who will share in this much deeper knowledge of God. It is only those to whom Jesus chooses to reveal this knowledge who have it. He will do this to anyone who comes to him in humble faith.

Martin Luther commented, 'Here the bottom falls out of all merit, all powers and abilities of reason, or the free will men dream of, and it counts for nothing before God; Christ must do and give everything.'

The work of the Holy Spirit is to reveal the truth about Jesus
Read John 16:13-15

[Space forbids any serious treatment of the work of the Holy Spirit in salvation in this book. But these verses show that the work of the Holy Spirit is to guide into all truth. As Jesus had previously declared, 'I am... the truth' (John 14:6), a vital aspect of the work of the Holy Spirit is to make him known.]

Anyone who rejects Jesus does not have eternal life
Read John 3:36

What about the unevangelised?

It will help us to clarify our thinking about the unevangelised if we distinguish various groups amongst them. It is important to remember that we are referring to those who, through no fault of their own, have not heard the gospel in a way which is *meaningful* to them, and so have not *rejected* it. Many millions have heard the gospel and, sadly, deliberately or in effect, rejected it. The New Testament holds out no hope in the case of deliberate rejection of known truth.

Those from other religions or none who have not heard the gospel and are not seeking the truth
Amongst these are:

i. Some of those who are convinced (or apathetic) atheists. According to Romans 1, there is no excuse for their rejection of the revelation of God in creation.

ii. Some apathetic agnostics. Again there is no excuse for this position.

iii. Some nominal followers of other religions. They worship merely out of tradition or duty. Or they merely use religion in a rather superstitious way for their own personal benefit. This will include nominal Christians. They are making no effort to seek a proper relationship with God. It is arguable that this group forms a large proportion of the world's population.

iv. Some sincere but contented followers of other religions. They regard their religion as important and are convinced of its truth. They participate in religious observance out of conviction, but they are content to stop at that. They are not earnestly seeking a deeper relationship with God which goes beyond their current religious experience and context. We have no biblical mandate for regarding any of this group as saved.

Groups i. to iv. may account for the majority of unevangelised people. They are not responding to the revelation of God they have received by earnestly seeking a deeper relationship with him, which goes beyond their current religious experience and context. Such apathy is inexcusable and, if it continues, the people concerned must accept responsibility for the consequences. If they are ultimately unsaved there can be no question of this raising doubts about the love and justice of God.

Those from other religions or none who have not heard the gospel but are earnestly and consistently seeking a deeper relationship with God

1. What does the OT say about those who seek God in the following verses:

1 Chron 28:9

Prov 8:17

Is 55:6

There are many other OT passages which give hope to those who seek Yahweh, although they are addressed to the people of Israel.

2. What did Jesus say about those who seek God?

Mt 7:7-8

3. There is even more hope in Hebrews 11:6. Write out this verse:

Biblical evidence about how God deals with the unevangelised who are seeking him

Jews before Christ

On what grounds was Abraham accepted by God?

Rom 4:3

The main argument in Romans 1-8 is that we are accepted by God through faith in Jesus. Abraham could not have known about Jesus, yet God accepted him according to the faith he had in God's revelation up to that point. We can be sure that this applied to all Jews before Christ who had a similar heart attitude to that of Abraham.

Gentiles before Christ

According to Romans 1, those who reject God's revelation in creation are without excuse. But what hint is given in the following verses about those who are in ignorance yet truly seek God:

Acts 17:27

Acts 17:30

It seems from these passages that in the case of those Gentiles before Christ who understood that they depended on God for their very existence, and put themselves out to seek him, he would overlook the ignorance which caused them to have man-made images, and hints that they may find him.

(For more information on Acts 17 see For Further Study section.)

Gentiles after Christ (Acts 10:1-11:18)

Cornelius was a Roman centurion from a pagan background.

1. How is Cornelius described?

Acts 10:2,22

2. What revelation did he experience?

Acts 10:3-6

3. Why did God give this revelation?

Acts 10:4

4. What was the purpose of the revelation?

Acts 10:22; 11:14

5. What did Cornelius want to hear from Peter?

Acts 10:33

6. How did Peter respond to the spirituality of Cornelius?

Acts 10:34-35

Cornelius was a 'God-fearer' (Acts 10:2). This is a technical Jewish term for a Gentile 'who was not a full Jewish proselyte but who believed in one God and respected the moral and ethical teaching of the Jews' (NIV Study Bible). He is therefore an example of people from a non-Christian background who are obedient to the spiritual light they have received. They are earnest seekers after God. Their heart attitude is pleasing to God who, whilst he gives salvation by grace, judges human beings according to works. They are God fearers. Gerhard Krodel defines the fear of God helpfully. He says, 'Fear of God is not the feeling of terror of the transcendent, but the recognition that God expects to be honoured, that his will is to be fulfilled, that he remains the impartial judge and that in prayer we may address him.'[2]

However, Cornelius did hear the gospel. When was he saved?

Acts 11:14

He was not saved until he received the gospel through Peter's preaching, and the gift of the Holy Spirit. Non-Christians are not saved by their sincerity. But to have an attitude like that of Cornelius predisposes a person to receive the gospel. And God responded in Cornelius' case by ensuring that he heard the gospel. The angel could have proclaimed the gospel to him, but it was important that Peter was involved to break down the barrier between Jews and Gentiles.

(For Further material on Cornelius see For Further Study section.)

Jews after Christ

1. How does Paul describe his attitude to God before his conversion?

Acts 22:3

2. What was his attitude to Judaism before his conversion?

Gal 1:14

3. How does Paul describe his fulfilment of the law before his conversion?

Phil 3:6b

4. How did Paul react to Stephen's proclamation of the gospel?

Acts 7:59-8:1

5. What was Paul's attitude to Christians as he set out for Damascus?

Acts 9:1

Even though Paul had rejected the gospel and was viciously persecuting the church, Jesus appeared to him (Acts 9:3-6) and brought him to faith in him. This encourages us to believe that even those who are antagonistic to Christianity may be brought to faith in Christ through direct, divine intervention, without human involvement, as long as they make a positive response.

In the story of Cornelius the angel could easily have conveyed the Gospel to him. We must not limit God's work to the church and evangelism. If a supernatural revelation can be given to Cornelius, as a pagan who had not heard the gospel but was earnestly and consistently seeking a deeper relationship with God, the same can happen to others. There is considerable recent evidence that this is so.

People from other faith backgrounds testify to coming to know Christ by direct revelation rather than through evangelism or background knowledge of Christianity. God in his grace reaches out to those who are unevangelised.

That is no excuse for not evangelising: the Lord commands us to do that. But it is an encouragement when thinking of the many who have never heard the gospel in a way which is meaningful to them. It is important to stress though that salvation is through Christ, not through religion or good deeds.

There will remain unanswered questions about the unevangelised. We must ultimately trust in God's love and justice. He will deal with them perfectly. 'Will not the Judge of all the earth do right?' (Gen 18:25).

SUMMARY

1. Eternal life is knowing God the Father and Jesus Christ.

2. Unbelievers do not know God.

3. General revelation makes it inexcusable not to know about God.

4. Knowing the Father requires revelation by Christ.

5. The work of the Holy Spirit is to reveal the truth about Jesus.

6. Anyone who rejects Jesus does not have eternal life.

But, what of those who have never heard the Gospel?

1. No hope is held out for those who do not trouble to seek the truth or who reject God's revelation.

2. There are small hints in the New Testament about a positive attitude to Gentiles who were true seekers before Christ.

3. We know that Jews who had true faith in God's revelation of himself were justified by faith before Christ.

4. God revealed Jesus to Paul without human intervention.

We should therefore trust in the justice and mercy of God. Scripture teaches that God had mercy on Jews before Christ came, if they were truly seeking Yahweh in faith. Our view is that God, who is outside time, was able to show mercy on the basis of the sacrifice of the Lamb of God 'who was slain from the creation of the world' (Rev 13:8). It is possible that, on the same basis, God had mercy on Gentiles who were truly seeking him before Christ.

We can also be confident that since the time of Jesus the Holy Spirit has revealed him to some, perhaps many, without human intervention. There is hope therefore for true seekers who are unevangelised, or even those who are not seekers if they respond to God's revelation in Christ.

Christians should be definite where Scripture is (especially that God only saves us on the basis of Christ's sacrifice); trust in the nature of God where there are unanswered questions; and above all obey Jesus' last command in Matthew 28:18-20.

[NB.A hint that God may deal differently with children who die before reaching the age of discretion may be in 1 Corinthians 7:14. There Paul calls the children of believers 'holy', which means set apart, in a covenant relationship with God. If this is the case then it may apply to others, such as the mentally handicapped, who have not reached the age of discretion. We must trust children who do not have a believing parent to the mercy of God.]

> ### *GROUP DISCUSSION*
> Discuss the Summary (above). Does it describe your beliefs or answer some of your questions?

Notes

1. Quoted in Netland *op.cit.* pp270ff.

2. G. A. Krodel, *Augsburg Commentary on the New Testament, Acts* (Augsburg: Minneapolis), 1986, p196.

FOR FURTHER STUDY

Matthew 11:27

Dr Leon Morris, *The Gospel according to Matthew* (Eerdmans: Grand Rapids, 1992), pp294ff, comments on Matthew 11:27, 'Jesus is saying that his knowledge of the Father surpasses that in any revelation made hitherto: he knows the Father as he really is. He has a knowledge of the Father not shared by any of his contemporaries. To this he adds, 'and the one to whom the Son wills to reveal him.' This does not mean that those who receive the revelation know the Father in the same intimate way as the Son does. Knowledge that springs from community of nature is not the same as that which comes from revelation. It means rather that it is in him that they come to know God. Those who are willing to receive the revelation in Jesus will have a knowledge of God not open to anyone else. Notice that the revelation is connected with the will of the Son. The revelation of the Father does not come by chance; it comes only to those to whom the Son chooses to make the revelation. The saying ascribes to Jesus the critical place in the revelation of the Father.'

Morris adds the following footnotes:

'*epiginoskei*. The verb is sometimes held to have the meaning "know fully, exactly," but this is not easy to prove. J Armitage Robinson has a lengthy examination of this verb and its cognate noun (*St Paul's Epistle to the Ephesians* [London, 1907], pp248-54) in which he finds *gnosis* to be the wider word with *epignosis* knowledge directed towards a particular object. We should notice that in the Lucan parallel the verb is *ginosko*.'

'*ho ean* is general, "to whomever"; Jesus is not claiming to found an exclusive set of gnostics, people with special spiritual endowment. His revelation is open to anyone who comes humbly. It is not easy to get an idiomatic English equivalent, and a number of translations bring out the universal aspect by rendering with a plural, "to those whom..."'

'The verb *boulomai* (which Matthew uses only twice) signifies a decision of the will, often after deliberation. There is no thought of capriciousness.'

Robert W Mounce, *New International Biblical Commentary, Matthew* (Hendrickson, Peabody: Massachusetts, 1991), pp107-108, comments, 'The authenticity of the verse is regularly questioned because of its Johannine ring (cf John 3:35; 10:15). Other obstacles are the absolute use of the title *the Son* and the claim of mutual personal knowledge, which suggests Gnostic and Hermetic influence. Bultmann calls the passage a "Hellenistic revelation saying" (*History of the Synoptic Tradition*, p159). Similarity, however, does not prove dependence. Until it is conclusively proven that the Fourth Gospel is a later stage in christological thought, we need not be surprised if at places the words of Jesus in the Synoptics sound somewhat like his words in John. The absolute use of "the Son" in Mark 13:32 (hardly a copyist's emendation, in that it claims ignorance of the time of the Parousia on the part of Jesus) answers one problem, and the emphasis on knowledge in the Dead Sea Scrolls answers the other. Jeremias points out the number of Semitisms that argue an early date and thus strengthen the case for authenticity (*NT Theology, vol.1*, pp57-59).

CORNELIUS

Rev Thomas Walker, *The Acts of the Apostles* (Moody: Chicago, 1965), pp240ff, comments, 'Cornelius represents a class who, though ignorant of the Gospel, honestly seek to live up to their light and to act on the dictates of their conscience (cf Rom 2:10-16). Obedient to the truth, so far as he knew it, he had renounced idolatry and become a sincere worshipper of the one true God and an earnest seeker after still clearer light. When that light shined on him he readily accepted it and basked in its radiance. We are not to isolate the expression from its context, but to view it in its proper setting and proportion. Those who quote Cornelius' example as illustrating their own spiritual position must show his readiness to seek the way of life and to accept with gladness the Gospel of Christ... The idea expressed is that the disposition of heart evidenced by Cornelius and men of his type is one which God can regard with favour, so as to meet and satisfy it... Though the centurion was not yet actually in a state of salvation (11:14) he was an earnest seeker after it. And those who seek shall find (Mt 7:7-8). As Bengel says, what is predicated here is indifference to a man's nationality, not indifference as to the nature of the religion which he professes.'

Note, however, that it is not said that Cornelius was accepted because of his good works—they were simply evidence of his spirituality.

Professor F. F. Bruce, *The Acts of the Apostles*, Greek Text, (Apollos: Leicester, 1990), p261, makes a very important point, 'While divine salvation is according to grace (cf 15:11), the undeviating principle in divine judgment is "to everyone according to his works" (cf Rom 2:6; Rev 20:12ff), and is so stated throughout the Bible, from Gen 4:7 ("If you do well, will you not be accepted?") to Rev 22:12 ("I am coming...to repay everyone for what he has done."). Peter's statement (Acts 10:34-35) that in every nation those who fear God and do what is right are accepted by him is of great importance in introducing the role of God-fearing Gentiles in Luke's account of the expansion of Christianity.'

David J. Williams, *New International Bible Commentary, Acts* (Hendrickson, Peabody: Massachusetts, 1985), p192, comments, '...a person's acceptance with God rested, not on nationality, but on proper disposition of heart: he "accepts men from every nation who fear him and do what is right" (v35). This is not to say that nothing else is needed. The emphasis on Jesus in this speech gives the lie to this. Jesus is integral to our salvation. Rather, what Peter meant is that if the attitude is right, then given the Good News, there is no-one who cannot be saved.'

Everett F. Harrison, *Acts: The Expanding Church* (Moody: Chicago, 1975), p172, says, 'God is prepared to receive those "in every nation" who fear him and work righteousness, the very things which are noted about Cornelius (10:2 cf Matt 6:1-2). The meaning is not that such persons are thereby saved (cf Acts 11:14) but rather are suitable candidates for salvation: such preparation betokens a spiritual earnestness which will result in faith as the Gospel message is heard and received.'

Dr J. R. W. Stott, *The Bible Speaks Today, The Message of Acts* (IVP: Leicester, 1990), pp198ff, writes, 'God is represented as being pleased with [Cornelius]. His prayers and gifts had "come up as a memorial offering before God" (10:4,31). This phrase "memorial offering" translates *mnemosynos*, a sacrificial word used in the LXX of the so-called "memorial portion" of an offering which was burned. Does this mean that Cornelius' prayers and alms had been "accepted as a sacrifice in the sight of God" (31, *Jerusalem Bible*)? And what did Peter mean when he states that God "accepts" (*dektos*) in every nation those "who fear him and do what is right" (10:35)?'

Stott says that one possibility is that *dektos* means 'justification' and is referring to believers, irrespective of their race or rank. But he continues, 'An alternative explanation, however, seems to me to fit the context better. This is that *dektos* means not "accepted" in the absolute sense of justified, but "acceptable" in a comparative sense, because in everybody God prefers righteousness to unrighteousness and sincerity to insincerity, and in the case of Cornelius God provided for him to hear the saving gospel.

'What Peter emphatically did not mean is that anyone of any nation or religion who is devout ("fears God") and upright ("does right") is thereby justified. Calvin rightly dismisses this notion as "an exceedingly childish error". [Calvin, I, p288]. Not only does it contradict Paul's gospel, which Luke faithfully records in Acts, but it is refuted in the rest of the Cornelius story. For this devout, God-fearing, upright, sincere and generous man still needed to hear the gospel, to repent (11:18) and to believe in Jesus (15:7). Only then did God in his grace (15:11) save him (11:14, 15:11), give him forgiveness of sins (10:43), the gift of the Spirit (10:45; 15:8) and life (11:18)...'

R. C. H. Lenski, *The Interpretation of the Acts of the Apostles* (Augsburg Publishing House: Minneapolis, 1961), pp418ff, comments on v35, '... *ho theos* is the true God who reveals himself in the Scriptures and not God as some imagine him... No greater insult can be offered to God than to disregard his Word concerning himself and our relationship to him. In no way does Peter say or imply that a pagan who is serious about what he is pleased to call god is accepted by God.'

Dr P. J. Gloag, *A Critical and Exegetical Commentary on the Acts of the Apostles, Vol.1* (Klock and Klock: Minneapolis; T & T Clark: 1870, reprinted 1979), p378, quotes Neander (Planting, Vol. i. pp74,75) on verse 35,

'As to these memorable words of Peter... the sense cannot be, that in every nation, every one who only rightly employs his own moral power will obtain salvation: for had Peter meant this, he would, in what he added, announcing Jesus as Him by whom alone men could obtain forgiveness of sin and salvation, have contradicted himself. But evidently Peter spoke in opposition to the Jewish nationalism: God judges men not according to their descent or non-descent from the theocratic nation, but according to their disposition. All who, like Cornelius, honour God uprightly, according to the measure of the gift entrusted to them, are acceptable to Him; and He prepares by His grace a way for them, by which they are led to faith in Him who alone can bestow salvation.'

Dr Rudolph Stier, *The Words of the Apostles*, translated from the second German edition by G. H. Venables (T & T Clark: Edinburgh, 1869), pp165ff, comments, '(Peter) had considered that even a Gentile thus prepared (as Cornelius was) was excluded on account of his uncircumcision, and had been in error not only as to the preparing, but also as to the perfecting grace of God...'

'And outward adhesion to the Israel of God, as in the case of Cornelius, is not the only way in which a heathen can actually fear God, but because the true God nowhere leaves Himself entirely without a witness among the heathen (ch xiv. 17), because the mysterious and yet widespread sound of Him has gone forth into all lands, and His high-sounding but yet voiceless words to the very end of the earth (Rom 10:18 if correctly interpreted), therefore can men everywhere, in some way or other, although in very different degrees, manifest awe and fear of this divine testimony with an accompanying obedient belief, and can consequently have in the heart the rudiment of the true religion completed in Christ....'

'As regards the blind perversion of the whole question, which asserts that equality of religion for all nations, and a complete righteousness for the heathen without Christ, are therein taught, it scarcely needs mention here. Against this idea it might be simply said, "Cornelius might thus have always remained a mere heathen."...Only by Satan's craft can these words be thus torn away from their context.'

R. B. Rackham, *Westminster Commentaries, The Acts of the Apostles* (Methuen: London, 1910), pp155ff, writes, 'In the sixteenth century, led away by reaction against exaggerated merit attached to good works, with minds dominated with the idea of justification by faith and by St Paul's words, "whatsoever is not of faith is sin," extreme reformers denied the possibility of any righteousness before justification...Cornelius...was already working righteousness and acceptable to God, before he had consciously "believed in Christ". But he was not therefore without the inspiration of the Spirit of Christ. For as St Augustine says (*Ep.* 194, 18), "the Spirit breathes where he wills...in one way he helps before indwelling, in another by indwelling. For before he indwells he helps men to become faithful, those already faithful he helps by indwelling." And, as we have seen, the Holy Spirit was at work in bringing about the conversion of Cornelius (verse 20). But, although acceptable to God, his righteousness was still imperfect. For it did not spring from the highest motive, viz. conscious faith in Christ, of whose work of redemption he was ignorant. It was then acceptable to God in the sense that it predisposed him for justification. Not that even thus it had any merit. The mission of the angel and of St Peter came of God's pure mercy. The outpouring of the Spirit was a free "gift", Cornelius had not earned that mercy, his goodness was rather a sign that he was ready to receive it. There were many others at that moment among the Gentiles working righteousness, but only Cornelius was selected by God for this conversion. To inquire further why God chooses this particular person or that is to lose ourselves in the inscrutable mysteries of the Divine Being.... Cornelius had not as yet obtained the full light or eternal life, ie the knowledge of God. But his natural goodness had fitted him to receive "the word," which God of his free grace now sent him...'

J. B. Polhill, *The New American Commentary, Vol. 26, Acts* (Broadman: Nashville, Tennessee, 1992), pp260ff, comments, 'Was God responding to Cornelius' works, "rewarding", so to speak, by bringing Peter with the saving gospel and granting him his gift of the Spirit? One must be careful not to introduce Paul's theology into a context that is not dealing with the same issues, but one should note that even Paul was capable of describing the impartial justice of God as based on one's good or evil works (Rom 2:9-11). The early church fathers struggled with the question of faith and works in Cornelius, and perhaps Augustine's view offers as good an answer as any. Cornelius, like Abraham, had shown himself to be a man of faith and trust in God. God was already working his grace in him, and it manifested itself in his good deeds. Now God would show him his greatest grace in the gospel of Jesus Christ and the gift of the Spirit. The stress on both Cornelius' devoutness and his works is perhaps, then, a good corrective to an abused doctrine of grace with no implications for behaviour and a reminder of James's dictum that at base, faith and works are inseparable.'

Professor F. L. Arrington, *The Acts of the Apostles* (Hendrickson, Peabody: Massachusetts, 1988), pp112ff, believes Cornelius and his friends were already converted before Peter met them, but this does not seem to fit the context. He comments: 'Devout people like Cornelius and his friends would know about the public ministry of Jesus that had begun in Galilee with the baptism of John the Baptist (v37). However the words "you know"...seem to indicate that not only were these God-fearing Gentiles acquainted with the ministry of Jesus but they were already converted. Based on the narrative of Acts we could assume that the people of Cornelius heard the first Christian sermon from Peter, but Philip the Evangelist lived in Caesarea (8:40; 21:8). He or some other Christian could have introduced them to the gospel...nothing is mentioned by Peter concerning the repentance or conversion of Cornelius and his people. At the conclusion of his sermon Peter declared that everyone who believes in Christ receives forgiveness of sins (v43). This theme is not given prominence in the sermon, and the sermon does not close with a call to repentance. Thus the preaching of Peter did not result in the conversion of these Gentiles. They were already saved...'

Summary of implications drawn from the story of Cornelius

Walker makes the important point that, as Jesus said, those who seek (God), like Cornelius, will find (him). This is not because of good works for they are merely evidence of spirituality. Similarly Harrison speaks of Cornelius' attitude as 'spiritual earnestness' which will result in faith when the gospel is heard and received. Gloag takes a similar line.

Stott points out that God prefers righteousness and sincerity to unrighteousness and insincerity, including in those who have not yet come to faith in Christ. Equally important is Bruce's statement that, whereas salvation is by grace, judgment in scripture is always according to works. Polhill reminds us of the inseparability of faith and works—faith without works is dead. Hence Cornelius was acceptable to God in what Stott calls a comparative way rather than in the deeper sense of justification.

Lenski is right to emphasise that to have this comparative acceptability a God-fearer must be serious about the true God ie. Yahweh, not about some so-called god.

Rackham uses unwise terminology which seems not entirely to avoid the idea of meriting justification, even though he specifically denies such an idea. He speaks of Cornelius' goodness 'predisposing him to justification'. He also speaks of his natural goodness fitting him to receive the word. Any idea of justification by works is, of course, contradictory to the NT.

ACTS 17

The Church of England report, *Multi-Faith Worship?*, para 39, says, 'Paul makes a positive evaluation of the "religiousness" of the Athenians, and quotes from what may be regarded as their sacred Scriptures, the Poets...he makes the "unknown" known, and condemns idolatry— but neither does he wish judgment upon the Athenian religion to be purely negative. Their religious traditions, it might be claimed, were in part a response to the calling of the unnamed, cosmic Christ, and as such were regarded as part of God's gracious preparation for the full proclamation of the Gospel. Paul's judgment did not entail a general positive evaluation of other worship traditions, so much as a spiritual discernment that the hearts of those he encountered in Athens were by no means entirely turned away from God by their religious observances.'

In our view, this statement is overly positive, but nevertheless there is a hint in Acts 17:27 and 30 of a positive attitude to those who worshipped idols in ignorance but were seeking God.

ROMANS 2:12-16

As we have already noted, this passage speaks of the law being written on the hearts of unbelieving Gentiles. Some claim it shows there is salvation apart from Christ. However v16 states that Christ will be the criterion of judgment on the Day of Judgment. The whole purpose of the passage is that both Jews and Gentiles have failed to keep the law and are without excuse. Nevertheless, the passage shows that God has not left himself without a witness in unbelievers. Many of them do respond positively to the 'inner law'. This can lead some of them to the attitude Cornelius displayed.

EPHESIANS 2:12

E. F. Scott, *The Epistles of Paul to the Colossians, to Philemon and to the Ephesians, Moffat NT Commentary* (Hodder & Stoughton: London, 1948), p170, comments on Ephesians 2:12, 'All the piety of the Gentiles was bounded by the material world. They had no knowledge of the God who made it and by fellowship with whom they would be raised above it. Even their so-called "gods" were beings of the created world.'

Professor T. K. Abbott, *International Critical Commentary, The Epistles to the Ephesians and the Colossians* (T & T Clark: Edinburgh, 1897), p59, writes, 'They were truly "without God", as not knowing him. Notwithstanding their many gods, they had no conception of a Creator and governor to be loved and trusted. So far as their consciousness was concerned, they had no God...This was not the occasion for referring to the noble exceptions to the moral degradation of heathenism.'

Andrew T. Lincoln, *Word Biblical Commentary Vol 42, Ephesians* (Word Books: Dallas, 1990), p138, says,'The

Gentile readers may have believed in a god or gods, but they did not have the true God, Israel's God.'

EVANGELICAL VIEWS

Harold Netland, *op.cit.*, pp265-76, outlines a spectrum of Evangelical views on the unevangelised as follows:

a. *Those who believe salvation is only through conscious, explicit faith in Christ.* This, of course, means all those who have never heard the gospel are lost. The apparent implication is that this means all those in the OT are lost too. However some say the OT saints were in an exceptional situaton because they received special revelation (which included divinely-appointed sacrifice). On believing it they were saved. Some believe that God will give everyone who sincerely seeks him an opportunity to hear the gospel.

b. *Those who believe God has ways of dealing with the unevangelised who are seeking him, which we don't know about.* They will be judged according to how they respond to the light they have received. However salvation would be on the basis of grace not works. Such people would need to cast themselves on the mercy of God.

c. *Those who draw a parallel between the unevangelised and the people of the OT.* This view holds out the possibility of salvation without explicit faith in Christ. Again, as with the OT saints, salvation is implicitly by grace through Christ.

d. *Those who hold that people are given a chance to respond to the gospel at or soon after death.*

CHAPTER 9 | WHAT ABOUT INTERFAITH COOPERATION?

We live in a global village. With modern travel and telecommunications we are all likely to have contact with people of other faiths. Then there is the growth of militant fundamentalism amongst Muslims, which is a major political factor on the world scene and, to a lesser extent, is to be seen amongst Hindus and Buddhists (and sadly amongst some nominal Christians, eg in N. Ireland). This all raises the question:

What should be our attitude to people of other Faiths?

1. How does Jesus answer the question?

Mt 22:39

2. What about extreme religious fundamentalists who persecute believers? List the responses Jesus commands.

Lk 6:27-36

3. What was Jesus' attitude to the Samaritans in the following passages?

Lk 9:51-55

Lk 10:29-37

Lk 17:11-19

Jn 4:7-9

This contrasts with the attitude of the Jews of the time who despised the Samaritans as a mixed-blood race. During the exile Israelites who remained in Israel had intermarried with Gentiles whom the Assyrians had exiled to Israel. There were major religious differences between them and the Jews, so the Jews did not associate with Samaritans. This explains the Samaritans' refusal to welcome Jesus in Luke 9:53.

Jewish rabbis would rarely be seen talking in public to a *Jewish* woman, let alone a Samaritan woman. Also a Jew would become ceremonially unclean if he used a cup handled by a Samaritan. The Jews regarded the Samaritans as permanently ceremonially unclean.

Christians should not want to encourage and facilitate people in activities which are contrary to the gospel and teaching of scripture. But they should respect the rights and freedom of people of other faiths.

What about inter-faith dialogue?

What did Paul do in the following passages?

Acts 17:16-17

Acts 19:8-10

These were situations of discussion and dialogue but, no doubt, with an explicit evangelistic purpose. There is nothing in scripture to forbid more general inter-faith dialogue. It is a way of discovering about people of other faiths, which helps to know how to pray for them, show the love of Christ to them and share the gospel with them. Jesus certainly knew about Samaritan religion and Paul about Greek religion, and this facilitated their evangelism. (We do not recommend entering into dialogue if you are not knowledgeable and convinced about the Christian faith. To do so could lead to confusion).

There are two important conditions for dialogue. Without fulfilling them, Christians could confuse people of other faiths and hinder them responding to the gospel. The conditions are:

a. It should be clear to both sides that the dialogue, whilst based on mutual respect between the participants, is not based upon Christians regarding both religions as equally true.

b. It should be clear to both sides that the Christian participants, whilst not manipulating, pressurising or otherwise showing disrespect for the other participants, nevertheless want them to come to faith in Christ. Many people of other faiths welcome this honesty.

It is, of course, possible for Christians to cooperate with people of other faiths over social, moral, community and political issues. Often there is much in common between the different faith groups and they can work together as responsible citizens.

[For more material on dialogue see For Further Study section.]

Should we evangelize people of other Faiths?

1. What did Jesus say to a sincere Jewish leader?

Jn 3:3-8,14-15

2. What did Jesus say to the Samaritan woman (who had her own religion)?

Jn 4:10,13-14

3. What frank statement did Jesus make to her?

Jn 4:22

4. What did Paul say to the Athenians (who had their own religion)?

Acts 17:30-31

It is clear from this study that people of other faiths need to come to faith in Christ. It follows that, lovingly and sensitively, Christians should evangelise them.

Can we pray together with people of other Faiths?

Some claim that people of different religions are all worshipping the same God. Whereas it may be true that many millions are reaching out to the one true God, that is a very different matter from coming to know God through revelation, and to be known by him.

a. How do we have access to God

1. What is Jesus according to Paul?

1 Tim 2:5

(see also Heb 8:6; 9:15; 12:24)

2. How do we approach God according to the following passages?

Eph 2:18

Eph 3:12

3. What gives us access to God according to the following passages?

Eph 2:13

Col 1:19-20

4. What regulation about worship was the high priest obliged to keep?

Heb 9:7

5. What is the parallel to this in the ministry of Jesus?

Heb 9:11-12

6. What alone cleanses those who draw near to worship God?

Heb 10:1-10

(NB. The phrase 'the blood of Christ' refers to the violent death of Jesus for our sins.)

The Bible teaches that true worship and prayer (drawing near or having access to God) are only possible through the blood of Christ and through faith in him. This is the heart of the gospel and is not negotiable for Christians. That is not to say that God never hears the prayers of non-Christians. But when he does it is still because of the blood of Christ.

Multi-faith worship inevitably marginalises (or sometimes even excludes any explicit reference to) Christ:

a. By appearing to set him alongside other deities, saviours or ways of salvation.

b. By encouraging people to worship God in a way which ignores or marginalises Christ.

c. By undermining the truth that access to God (even by the prayers of non-Christians) is only through Christ.

In other words, multi-faith worship undermines or contradicts the gospel.

b. What responsibility do we have for those of other faiths?

1. What principle is to be observed by the strong believer?

1 Cor 8:9-13

Paul is primarily concerned here with the damage that a strong believer eating in an idol's temple might do to a more vulnerable Christian believer. That is a relevant consideration in connection with multi-faith worship.

Equally, it is unloving to cause people of other faiths to stumble and be hindered in responding to the gospel by our involvement in multi-faith worship. If we are marginalising Christ as outlined above, we are damaging those of other faiths or of weak Christian faith, who are involved with us. That is unloving and unbiblical.

2. What are believers urged to do concerning those in error?

Jas 5:19-20

Again, this is referring to Christian believers who have fallen into error. But it surely has relevance to our attitude to people of other faiths. We should want lovingly to correct their unbiblical views. Jesus corrected the views of the Samaritan woman and Paul corrected the views of the Athenians.

Multi-faith worship, however, tends to confirm them in their errors:

a. By marginalising Christ in the ways outlined above.

b. By appearing to legitimise the truth of other faiths by implying they have equal validity to Christianity. Again, this is unloving and unbiblical. Most religions, quite apart from other errors, give the false impression that we can reach God by human effort.

c. *What about spiritual dangers to Christians?*

1. What does Paul say about sacrifices to idols?

1 Cor 10:20

2. How does he describe believers who participate in such sacrifices?

1 Cor 10:20

3. How does this relate to Communion?

1 Cor 10:21

(See For Further Study section.)

The dangers to Christians involved in multi-faith worship may be more clearly seen by a brief analysis of world religions.

In Section 6 we acknowledged that other religions are partly a response to Yahweh's revelation in creation, so they contain genuine insights about him. They have, in some cases, been influenced by special revelation, especially Judaism and Islam which rely extensively on the Old Testament. However there are demonic influences in false religious views too (including amongst Christians who abandon the faith, 1 Tim 4:1).

We outline here six groups of religions (see Appendix 2 for an outline of four major religions):

i. The first group are *philosophies* rather than religions in the strict sense, because they teach only about how to live in the world rather than how to worship God or gods. Buddhism in its original form is an example of this. However the majority of followers are dissatisfied with just a philosophy and tend to combine it with the worship of idols or placating spirits. This may be seen in a country like Sri Lanka where many people follow a mixture of Buddhism and Hinduism. The continuation and revival of religious belief in communist countries is an example of how human beings cannot be satisfied with philosophy.

ii. The second group are *pantheistic religions*. Many gods are worshipped, as in the religions of ancient Greece and Rome. But some regard idols as a manifestation of one ultimate reality. All is one and one is all. God is identified with the universe. Some forms of Hinduism are in this group.

iii. *Animistic Religions*. Many tribal religions have a vague notion of a remote 'high god' but concentrate on placating spirits, many of them thought of as indwelling natural objects.

iv. *Occult Religions*. In some religions the devil is actually worshipped or evil invoked.

v. *Cults*. These are usually extreme and fanatical deviations from a major religion.

vi. *Monotheistic Religions* which teach there is only one God. The three great monotheistic religions are Christianity, Judaism and Islam. Judaism, after the time of Jesus and the destruction of the Temple, developed in many different ways from OT Judaism, and reacted strongly against teaching that Jesus is the Messiah. Islam honours Jesus as a prophet but reacted strongly against the teaching that he is the Son of God. This is a serious matter.

4. What does the apostle John teach?

1 Jn 4:3

There is the possibility, therefore, of participants in multi-faith worship coming, perhaps unconsciously, under demonic influence.

5. What does Paul say?

2 Cor 6:14-15

6. What does he say about believers relating to idols?

2 Cor 6:16-17

Paul probably had in mind false teachers in the church. Believers were to separate from them. It is clear that Paul mixed with people of other faiths for the purpose of evangelism (Acts 17). But actually to worship or pray with those of other religions (including their teachers) surely amounts to being 'yoked together with unbelievers' (in context, 'unbelievers' means those without saving faith in Christ). Inevitably it is having fellowship (as opposed to evangelizing, having dialogue with a view to evangelizing or cooperating over 'non-religious' matters).

(See For Further Study section.)

Christians should not be involved in multi-faith worship for the following reasons:

a. It marginalises (or excludes) Christ through whose blood alone human beings have access to God.

b. It consequently hinders those of other faiths from responding to the gospel by appearing to confirm them in their errors.

c. It can lead to participants coming, perhaps unwittingly, under demonic influence.

d. It contradicts the biblical teaching against believers being 'yoked together with unbelievers' (ie those who do not believe in Christ).

Furthermore it is not necessary to worship and pray together in order to have good, respectful relationships and to further peace and harmony in society. In any case, many people of other faiths do not want multi-faith worship and regard it as compromise. It is quite possible to celebrate occasions together in a secular venue.

ONE EXCEPTION

The authors would participate in an exceptional event when there has been a tragedy or deliverance affecting the whole community or nation. We would be prepared to have a commemoration or celebration on neutral ground, which included the various religious groupings participating in a silent vigil of prayer.

This does not imply, in our view, any acceptance of or compromise with other religions, but is an expression of the importance we attach to religious freedom (within proper limits) in our society, and the recognition of the need in exceptional circumstances for religious leaders to express the grief or joy of the community.

BEWARE RACISM

Because some religions are associated with ethnic minorities, opposition to multi-faith worship can be perceived as racist. Although this should never be the motive, the reaction of ethnic minorities is understandable, given the racism in society. Christians need to be sensitive to this and do what we can to counteract it. We can stress, for example, that Christianity is a thoroughly multi-racial faith. Also we have a Jewish saviour! Nevertheless, in view of the serious implications of multi-faith worship, we should continue to oppose it.

GROUP DISCUSSION

1. Are there any multi-faith worship events involving the Christian churches in your area? Is God calling you to take any action involving peaceful protest?

2. Are there any steps you can take to get to know people of other faiths and show the love of Christ to them?

FOR FURTHER STUDY

The Christian and idolaters

Dr Paul Barnett, *The Bible Speaks Today, The Message of 2 Corinthians* (IVP: Leicester, 1988), p130, writes, 'It is a specific and technical association with temple worship which the apostle forbids. For this reason it is doubtful that Paul would agree with Christians today attending interfaith services with Muslims or Hindus, for example, since that would mean being mismated with unbelievers.'

Dr Colin Kruse, *Tyndale NT Commentaries, 2 Corinthians* (IVP: Leicester, 1987), pp137ff, comments on 2 Corinthians 6:14-16, 'In 1 Corinthians 10:14-22 Paul speaks of participation in pagan worship as fellowship with demons, and his question, What accord has Christ with Belial?, probably reflects concern in the same area. In this case his fourth rhetorical question, Or what has a believer in common with an unbeliever?, would be best interpreted in relation to worship, and the call for separation which this whole passage makes should then be related not to the day to day contacts that believers have with unbelievers (cf 1 Cor 5:9-10), but to the matter of pagan worship.'

' "What agreement has the temple of god with idols?" This final question with its worship imagery offers extra support for the view that the earlier questions reinforce a call to have no involvement in pagan worship.... For we are the temple of the living God. Having emphasized the incompatibility of "the temple of God" and idols (v16a), Paul with this affirmation shows why the Christian community must not become involved in pagan worship: it is because its members constitute the temple of the living God.'

Professor C. K. Barrett, *A Commentary on the First Epistle to the Corinthians* (A & C Black: London, 1968), p237, comments on 1 Corinthians 10:20, '(Paul) was convinced that the image used in idolatrous worship was a block of wood or stone and nothing more; it was not anything in the world. At the same time he believed in the reality of an unseen spirit-world (the evidence is to be found in chapter after chapter; eg 2:6,8; 4:9; 5:5; 6:3; 8:5), and that idolatry was not merely meaningless but a positively evil thing. It was evil primarily because it robbed the true God of the glory due to him alone (cf Rom 1:23), but it was evil also because it meant that man, engaged in a spiritual act and directing his worship towards something other than the one true God, was brought into intimate relation with the lower, and evil, spiritual powers. Thus the harmful effect of idolatry was not the eating of food contaminated in a quasi-physical sense, but in the worshipper's committing himself to an evil though subordinate power...'

'...it is not the eating of sacrificial food (which Paul permits) but direct participation in idolatry that will separate the Christian from Christ, and no more than the Israelites of old will he escape; his sacraments will preserve him from the moral consequences of idolatry, and from rejection and retribution, no more than did theirs.'

Dialogue

Towards a Theology for Inter-Faith Dialogue (*op.cit.*), pp33ff, says, 'Christians may never surrender a commitment to mission though the monologue is a style which should be relegated to the colonial past.... All genuine dialogue has a dimension of mission. For some this will imply the eventual possibility that all will be converted to Christ; for others it will be sufficient that each participant in dialogue has fully and fairly borne witness to their faith so that each understands more about the commitment of the other.'

Harold Netland (*op.cit.*), pp234ff, quotes Harvey Cox as saying that often Christians regard the issue of Jesus to be so controversial in dialogue that they postpone discussing him, and sometimes never reach the issue at all. Cox regards this as dishonest and points out that 'frequently it is precisely the question of Jesus that non-Christian participants seem most eager to get to.'

Netland recommends Christians being involved in dialogue because:

a. It is following the example of Jesus and Paul.

b. It shows a willingness to take fellow human beings seriously.

c. It is essential for effective evangelism.

d. It is a mark of humility, sensitivity and common courtesy (pp297-299).

CHAPTER 10
HOW SHOULD WE RESPOND?

Be clear about the arguments

Briefly, the arguments of each section in this course are as follows:

Section 1. God is personal and loving, so he reveals himself to us—primarily through Jesus. The divinely-inspired and authoritative record of this revelation is in scripture. It reveals God as both loving and holy. His holiness reacts against sin, bringing judgment. The Bible describes this reaction as the wrath of God. So the way of salvation must relate to his holiness, wrath and judgment as well as to his love, mercy and forgiveness.

Session 2. The New Testament clearly shows Jesus as both human and divine. Indeed, Jesus himself claimed divinity.

Section 3. Salvation is deliverance from sin, death, Satan, hell and the wrath of God. It is also blessing: believers are chosen, justified, united, reborn, sanctified and reconciled in Christ. They are justified (declared righteous) by God in his grace because Jesus bore their sins and the divine punishment upon them. The required human response is repentance and faith. Union with Christ is visibly signified and sealed by baptism. Saving faith will show itself in good works.

Section 4. God is love. But his holiness and perfect justice demand that sin must be punished. Sinners are separated from the pure light of God. But, since God is the source of life, sin is inevitably punished by death. Only God, who alone is sinless, can therefore save mankind. But his perfect justice demands the death penalty. He could not take that penalty upon himself because he is immortal. So God became man, without ceasing to be God, in order to suffer a penal death. Hence the (unique and only) incarnation, death and resurrection of the Son of God was necessary as the only way to save sinful humanity.

Section 5. God reveals himself through creation and he blesses all humanity. Other religions are partly a response to this revelation and so contain genuine insights about him. Some, like Judaism and Islam, are also influenced by special revelation in scripture. But because other religions deny that Jesus is the Christ, the Son of God incarnate and only way to God, they are not salvific (they don't bring salvation). Contrary to the claims of some people, the Old Testament does not show a positive attitude towards other religions.

Section 6. The New Testament does not show a positive attitude to other religions either.

Section 7. Idolatry is condemned throughout Scripture. This includes the 'literalist' approach which believes the deity is totally contained in the image. But it also includes the 'incense-burner' approach which believes that the deity is to some extent present within the idol.

Section 8. Eternal life is knowing God the Father and Jesus Christ. This is only possible through faith in Christ. Perhaps most non-Christians in the world are either convinced (or apathetic) atheists, apathetic agnostics, nominal or sincere but contented followers of other faiths. They must accept responsibility for the spiritual results of their outlook. But there are also those who have not heard the gospel, yet are earnestly and consistently seeking a deeper relationship with God. It seems that the Holy Spirit has revealed Jesus to some, perhaps many, without human intervention.

There is hope therefore for those truly seeking God if they respond to his revelation in Christ.

Section 9. Christians are called to show love to people of other faiths. They may rightly join in honest, respectful inter-faith dialogue with them. But they are also called to share sensitively the gospel with them. However it is wrong for Christians to be involved in multi-faith worship and prayer because it marginalises or excludes Christ (the only way to God). It therefore also hinders people of other faiths coming to Christ.

Intolerance?

Some would say that this approach to people of other faiths is intolerant. One writer says, 'Exclusivism strikes more and more Christians as immoral. If the head proves it true, while the heart sees it as wicked, un-Christian, then should Christians not follow the heart?'[1]

The answer is that Christians should follow the teaching of God's word, even though it may conflict with human sentiment.

Tolerance does not mean accepting what others say is correct; it means accepting (in one sense) something one believes to be incorrect. The word tolerance cannot be applied to something one agrees with!

Intolerance means refusing to accept something one can and should accept. So it is not intolerant to say other faiths are wrong where they disagree with Scripture. Nor is it intolerant to seek to convey the gospel to people of other faiths or to avoid involvement in an inter-faith activity which conflicts with the teaching of Scripture. But it would be intolerant to refuse people the right to follow other faiths or to persecute them for doing so.

Recognize the urgency and importance of the subject

1. What spirit does John refer to in the following passage?

1 Jn 4:3

2. How long has this spirit been operating on earth?

1 Jn 4:3

3. How many antichrists are there?

1 Jn 2:18

There is, however, to be one ultimate incarnation of the antichrist spirit. It is described as 'the man of lawlessness' in 2 Thessalonians 2 and 'the Beast' in Revelation 13:1-10 (compare 1 John 2:18; 4:3)

4. What is the characteristic of the antichrist according to the following passages?

1 Jn 2:22-23

1 Jn 4:1-3

2 Jn 7

2 Thess 2:4

The spirit of antichrist has been in the world since New Testament times. It is implacably opposed to Christ and the salvation he brings. In many different ways down the centuries it has sought to undermine biblical teaching on the person and work of Christ. In our global village (a new phenomenon) with its yearning for peace, harmony and unity, the spirit of antichrist is manipulating the inter-faith movement, particularly in the area of multi-faith worship, to undermine the gospel. It seeks to deny that Jesus is the way, the truth and the life, and that no-one comes to the Father except through him. The purpose is to dishonour Christ and to prevent people coming to salvation. And it will get worse. We need to be vigilant against deceit and active in evangelism.

Meditate on the wonder of the gospel

We have a truly wonderful message—that God became man to die for our sins and to rise again so that those who repent and believe can be assured of eternal life and the resurrection of the body. He sends his Holy Spirit to give us power to live for him. Only in Christianity is such wonderful truth proclaimed.

Consider the following courses of action

1. Convey the teaching of this course to other Christians. Encourage other churches, groups and individuals to study the course. Remember young people at school who may be taught a multi-faith mishmash in Religious Education. Pray that Christians will get the message.

2. Clearly and prayerfully proclaim the uniqueness of Christ as the only Saviour to unbelievers. To know the truth is not enough: we must share it with others.

3. Be alert to multi-faith events etc., which may undermine the gospel. Pray about them and make appropriate peaceful protests (avoiding aggression, coercion and manipulation).

4. Support Christian organisations which evangelise

other faith groups. They are under pressure, including from the church.

5. Where possible, become involved with people of other faiths—sharing the love of Christ; discovering more about them and seeking to share the gospel with them.

6. Remember the danger of unintentionally giving a racist impression. Some readers may want to become involved with a truly Christian race-relations group—to become informed and to combat racism.

7. Whilst affirming the truth of Jesus the only Saviour, do not be afraid to say that we cannot answer all the questions raised by this belief.

8. Above all, through your worship and lifestyle, honour and glorify the Lord Jesus Christ, the only Saviour for the whole world who gave his life as a ransom for many.

Note

1. Quoted in Netland, *op.cit.*, p302.

APPENDIX 1 | EXCLUSIVISM, PLURALISM AND EPISTEMOLOGY

Exclusivism

Professor Harold A. Netland, *Dissonant Voices* (Apollos: Leicester 1991), p35, comments, 'What is often overlooked is that most, if not all, religious traditions are exclusivist... Most followers of any given religion regard their own religion as true and others which conflict with it as incomplete or false. Theravada Buddhists, for example, characteristically reject as false those claims made by Christians which are incompatible with Theravada Buddhism. Muslims reject as false those views about the prophet Muhammad which conflict with the teachings of Islam. Even Hinduism—widely hailed as the apotheosis of tolerance—is no exception. One finds in Shankara and Radhakrishnan vigorous arguments against those who do not accept their particular perspectives on reality.'

Professor Bikhu Parekh, *The Concept of Interfaith Dialogue* in *Many Mansions*, edited by Rabbi Dan Cohn-Sherbok (Bellew Publishing: London 1992), p164, similarly points out Hindu criticisms of Christianity. 'Hindu leaders... rejected the Christian conception of God on the grounds that it was relativistic and blasphemous, the former because it defined him from a narrow human point of view, the latter because it reduced him to the limited proportions of the human mind, attributed human emotions to him and detracted from his majesty.... The concept of a suffering God was unacceptably anthropomorphic and emotional. The doctrine of vicarious atonement violated the ideas of personal responsibility and just desert central to the Hindu doctrine of *Karma*.... The concept of mediation between man and God was logically and morally unnecessary and a likely source of much religious corruption. The idea that Jesus was the sole mediator was arrogant and impertinent and the source of Christian intolerance.'

Pluralism

Netland (*op.cit.*), pp201-233, gives a critique of the work of John Hick, one of the best-known pluralists. He tells us that Hick comes from a strongly evangelical background but has become God-centred rather than Christ-centred in his approach to religions. He distinguishes between the 'religious ultimate' as it is in itself and the religious ultimate as experienced by historically and culturally conditioned persons.

In spite of the great differences between religions (due, in his view, to this historical and cultural conditioning), Hick sees a common view of salvation amongst them. He defines it as a 'transformation from self-centredness to Reality-centredness' which shows itself in compassion, love, purity, inner peace, radiant joy etc.

Netland points out that if the different perceptions of the religious ultimate do not bear any relationship to the objective reality of the religious ultimate there seems little reason for referring to them as images of the ultimate reality. But if they do bear any relationship to the objective reality of the ultimate there are major problems. For example, how can the religious ultimate be described as both personal (as in Christianity) and impersonal (as in Buddhism and Hinduism)?

Hick affirms that much religious language about the religious ultimate is mythological. Netland responds that mythological statements about the religious ultimate 'are only informative to the extent that they are parasitic upon nonmythological—literal—truth' (p221). He continues that Hicks' theory does not account for the fact that each religious tradition regards its own view as the ultimate. He seems to favour the idea that the various views of God in the different religions are different names for the one ultimate. However he concedes that his theory would allow for these different views to be different gods, which leads to polytheism.

In order to support his theory, Hick re-interprets doctrines like the Incarnation in Christianity and the divine inspiration of the Quran in Islam as mythological, and virtually ignores the concept of special revelation. Netland points out that different religions interpret salvation very differently. Hick's definition—'Reality-centredness' would also be interpreted differently by them.

The conflicting truth-claims of the different religons cannot all be true. Netland informs us that Paul Knitter, a contemporary Roman Catholic theologian and pluralist, admits that the New Testament is exclusivist. 'Much of what the New Testament says is...*exclusive*, or at least *normative*.' Knitter continues, 'It is also either dishonest or naive to argue that the early Christians did not mean or believe what they were saying.... When the early Jesus-followers announced to the world that Jesus was the "one and only", they meant it' (quoted in Netland p251). However, like Hick, Knitter goes on to claim that such religious language is mythological.

Epistemology

It is beyond the scope of this course to deal with the issues of epistemology. However it is an important part of the debate on pluralism, as will be seen from the previous section. We therefore recommend Netland's book which is subtitled *Religious Pluralism and the Question of Truth*.

He points out that exclusivism is undermined in modern society by exposure to other faiths, epistemological skepticism, relativism and the distinction between public facts and private values (pp28-33). Other factors are a pragmatic assessment of religions in terms of what they do for adherents rather than their truth, the view that exclusivism is arrogant and intolerant and the growth of soteriological universalism.

He criticizes the pluralist emphasis on religious truth being non-propositional (pp126-133). He states that scripture refers to both propositional and non-propositional revelation. One cannot respond directly *to* God (non-propositional knowledge) without having some knowledge *about* him (propositional knowledge). In any case 'the most basic notion of truth in any realm whatsoever is propositional truth' (p129).

Pluralists who propound theories about religious truth being non-propositional are being self-contradictory. They are assuming that their religious theories are propositionally true!

Similarly, Netland provides a critique of the pluralist idea that religious truth is ineffable ie inexpressible (pp138-141). But to state that 'no meaningful statement can be made about God' is self-contradictory. Such a statement is itself a statement about God and so is meaningless!

Some proponents of the ineffability theory say that only negative statements can be made about God. But a negative predicate of God is only meaningful if there is presupposed some identifiable positive knowledge about God.

Finally, on pages 192ff, Netland gives ten epistemological criteria for evaluating religious traditions.

Conclusion

It is clear that most if not all religions are exclusive. And we argue in this book that, according to scripture, Christianity is exclusive rather than inclusive.

Pluralism, although growing in popularity, suffers from fatal weaknesses:

a. The most fundamental is that the truth claims of the various religions about the religious ultimate, salvation, etc., are mutually contradictory.

b. The pluralist tends to think that religious truth is non-propositional. But this is illogical. To have (non-propositional) knowledge *of* God requires having some (propositional) knowledge *about* God.

APPENDIX 1: EXCLUSIVISM, PLURALISM & EPISTEMOLOGY

c. The pluralist claim that statements about God are inexpressible is self-contradictory because that claim is in itself a statement about God.

APPENDIX 2 | MALACHI 1:11

J. A. Baldwin, *Haggai, Zechariah, Malachi, Tyndale NT Commentaries* (IVP: Leicester, 1972), pp227ff, comments on Malachi 1:11, 'The Hebrew needs no verb, and whether present or future tense is to be understood depends upon the verb in the next clause... "Incense" is offered' represents a difficult Hebrew expression made up of two participles, but (English Versions) solve the problem by taking the former as a noun "incense" (ie "that which is made to smoke"). The second, also passive and causative, means "is caused to be offered", though the tense is flexible and not necessarily present (cf AV, RV mgn, NIV "shall be" offered). The context has to be the decisive factor. But even if the future is used, it has the sense "is about to be offered", indicating that the event is near at hand and sure to happen. There is therefore an eschatological element in this verse.'

In a footnote Baldwin adds: 'A clear example of the Hoph'al participle having a future tense is in 2 Samuel 20:21, "shall be thrown".'

She continues that the adjective 'pure' is not used to describe Levitical offerings. 'To maintain that pagans could offer pure offerings to God when the God-given sacrifices are not so described is indefensible'. What Malachi is foreseeing is a worldwide acceptable worship, not dependent on the Levitical sacrifices, which Jesus was about to achieve through his sacrifice.

Prof J. M. P. Smith, *International Critical Commentary, Commentary on the Book of Malachi* (T & T Clark: Edinburgh, 1951), p31, comments that 'the allusions to the widely-scattered Jewish community (is) the most probable interpretation of the prophet's words. The view that this statement reflects the author's conviction that the gods of the heathen were only so many different names for the one great God and that the nations were in reality worshipping Yahweh finds many supporters. But against this is the following statement that incense is offered to Yahweh's name. Moreover the emphasis in Malachi upon ritualism and its attitude towards mixed marriages militate strongly against the hypothesis that its author could have taken so charitable and sympathetic a view of paganism.'

Smith thinks there is no grammatical evidence for a different dispensation (present to future) between verse 11 and verse 12.

R. L. Smith, *Word Biblical Commentary, Vol.32, Micah-Malachi* (Word Inc.: Waco, 1984), pp312ff, says that this verse 'is one of the most difficult verses in the OT to interpret'. He outlines five different interpretations:

a. The early Roman Catholic view that it is a prediction of the worldwide celebration of Communion. But, says Smith, this couldn't have been the original interpretation. And the verse seems to be referring to contemporary offerings.

It has to be said that Smith's criticism is unconvincing here. As we have seen, the verse may be prophetic. If it is, then it may not have been understood by Malachi's contemporaries, and it could refer to worldwide Christian worship.

b. That it refers to contemporary Jewish worship in the diaspora. Some Jewish commentators support this view. But nothing is said in this verse about Jewish worship outside Israel. And 'my Name is great among the nations' must surely refer to Gentile worship.

c. The syncretistic view that it refers to the worship of the high God in all religions. The majority of interpreters for the last hundred years have held this view. But Smith refers to Joyce Baldwin's refutation of it.

d. The view that the prophet is speaking metaphorically and using hyperbole, saying that some pagan worship is better than the current impure worship at Jerusalem. According to Smith 'this is a real possibility'.

e. That the verse is eschatological. This is the view of Joyce Baldwin.

Dr Rex Mason, *Cambridge Bible Commentary on the NEB, The Books of Haggai, Zechariah and Malachi* (CUP: 1977), pp144ff, adds a sixth interpretation. He parallels Malachi 1:11 to Psalm 50, the first verse of which contains the phrase 'from the rising of the sun to the place where it sets'. The psalm rejects animal sacrifice in favour of a sacrifice of thank offerings (v14) and of right living.

Mason points out that no blood sacrifices are mentioned in Malachi 1:11, but only incense offerings and cereal offerings. He says, 'The second of these can mean simply "a gift", as the NEB takes it. The reference may therefore be to the fact that when men anywhere acknowledge the mystery of creation and give thanks for it they are in fact acknowledging the greatness of the Creator's name (especially verse 14b).

Such worship, even if offered in ignorance of Yahweh's name, is more acceptable to him as offerings and gifts in their genuineness than the blood sacrifices offered by priests in the temple in a spirit of indifference.'

The NEB translates Malachi 1:11 as '... my name is held in awe among the nations.' The Hebrew is literally 'My name feared among the nations' and the NIV translates it 'My name is to be feared among the nations'. Mason comments on the NEB version, 'It is not meant that all nations worship Yahweh by name. Because he is king of all creation, however, when men worship the Creator they are really honouring Yahweh with a sincerity and zeal which shames the priests who claim to minister in his name.'

We should note, however, that:

i. The translation is uncertain.

ii. There is the possibility of hyperbole concerning pagan worship in reaction to indifferent and unacceptable Jewish worship.

iii. There is no inference made of other religions being salvific.

Dr Beth Glazier-McDonald, *Malachi—the Divine Messenger* (Society of Biblical Literature, Scholar's Press: Atlanta, 1987), pp57ff, refers to the interpretation that Malachi 1:11 refers to the zealous worship of Jewish proselytes throughout the diaspora. But because the law commanded that sacrifices could only be offered in Jerusalem these must have been spiritual sacrifices of praise and worship. Glazier-McDonald comments that the Hebrew for incense 'assumes real sacrifice' and that 'nothing is known about a vast movement of proselytes in this period.'

She opposes the syncretistic view that 'the gods of the nations were only so many different names for Yahweh, and that the nations were, therefore, in reality worshipping Yahweh'. She acknowledges that the verses before and after verse 11 refer to the present and some scholars have claimed that Persian influence on the returned exiles may have encouraged the idea of universal worship of one God.

However she quotes others who wonder 'how Malachi who attached such great importance to animal sacrifices, and who appeared so severe with regard to the negligence of the priests, could consider as sufficient compensation for the suppression of the cult at Jerusalem, the cult of the nations directed to the supreme deity. Indeed Malachi's negative attitude towards the Edomites, 1:2-5, and his condemnation of the abominations committed in Jerusalem, 2:10-16 (intermarriage, idolatry) "preclude a positive assessment of heathen religion" on his part (Rehm).'

Dr Glazier-McDonald gives some points in favour of the eschatological view:

i. 'From the rising of the sun to its setting' is a phrase often found in contexts which look to the future (Is 45:6; 59:19; Ps 50:1; 113:3).

ii. The role of universality in verse 11 and 14 that is so

striking 'belongs to the essential content of prophetic eschatology (Is 2:2f; 11:10f; 42:1-8; 45:1f,14f,22f; Mic 4:1ff; Zeph 3:8-9; Hag 2:7; Zech 8:20f; 14:16). In the prophetic vision, a time will come when Yahweh will be acknowledged as king (Mal 1:14; Zech 14:16; Ps 95-99) when the nations will join themselves to Yahweh (cf Is 14:1; Zech 2:11) and they will seek him in Jerusalem and entreat his favor (Mic 4:1f; Is 2:3f; 11:9; 42:4; 51:4; Jer 3:17; Zech 8:22).... To simply assert that Persian universalistic ideas have influenced the text is not satisfactory; it begs the question and overstates our knowledge of the nature and growth of Persian religion.... Moreover, because universalistic ideas can be traced far back in OT thought, there is no necessity to postulate borrowing from the Persians.' (pp60ff)

iii. 'It has been stated that noun-clauses, because of their verbless state, can describe only present conditions... On the contrary, the temporal reference of such clauses must be inferred from the context. Because the themes are futuristic the noun-clauses... may be said to point to a future fulfilment. Indeed it is not unusual for a participle, when it is the predicate of a noun-clause, to announce future action or events, especially if it is intended to announce the event as imminent, or at least near at hand and sure to happen (1 Kings 2:2; 2 Kings 4:16; Is 3:1; 7:14; Jer 30:20; Zech 2:13; 3:8)' (p61).

P. A. Verhoef, *The Books of Haggai and Malachi, New International Commentary on the OT* (Eerdmans: Grand Rapids, 1987), p230, accepts the possibility that the Jewish diaspora, proselyte diaspora and eschatological views are all true. 'The eschatological application of this text is but a continuation of its application to the Jews and proselytes... according to the character of prophecy, the beginning and the end, the first fruits and the full harvest, are being conceived as a whole.'

This is also the view of L Reinke, *Der Prophet Maleachi* (Gressen Ferber'sche Universitatsbuchhandlung: 1856), pp292ff.

Dr J. R. W. Stott, *The Bible Speaks Today, The Message of Acts* (IVP: Leicester, 1990), p198 note, writes, 'Some point to Isaiah 56:6ff. and Malachi 1:10-11 as teaching that God will accept the sacrifices of Gentiles. But in the former text the "foreigners" in view are those who bind themselves to Yahweh, love his name and hold fast to his covenant, while in the latter Yahweh rejects the offerings of Israel and instead accepts the offerings of those nations among whom his "name is great".'

Conclusion

We favour the eschatological view but recognize that it is not possible to be dogmatic. Clearly there is a strong case for rejecting any relevance to other religions.

APPENDIX 3 | OUTLINE OF THE MAIN WORLD FAITHS

It is not possible within the scope of this course to give a full description of the other main world faiths. But it would be incomplete without an outline of their main beliefs.

Hinduism

Hinduism is very diverse. It has no single doctrinal scheme and no single founder or prophet. Belief in God is not universal, nor are such beliefs as the world being illusory, vegetarianism or the caste system. However:

  a. Most believe in God (eg. Shiva, Vishnu or his avatars [incarnations] Krishna or Rama, or goddesses).

  b. They may believe in one God, or many, or the many as manifestations of the one God.

  c. Ultimate reality may be personal or impersonal.

  d. Almost all believe in Atman (the Eternal Self).

  e. Almost all believe in Samsara (the cycle of birth, reincarnation and transmigration of souls). This entails belief in karma which refers to work or action and its consequences. Moksha is release from the cycle of rebirth.

Scriptures

The main ones are the *VEDAS* (songs of knowledge) which are almost universally accepted as authoritative. They include:

  i. The Rigveda: 1028 hymns about 33 gods (from 1200 BC).

ii. The Samaveda: a handbook for shamans (witchdoctors).

iii. Yajurveda: a book of rituals, spells, and riddles.

iv. Atharvaveda: a book of hymns, spells, incantations concerning demons and philosophical speculation.

Then there are the *BRAHMANAS*. These include a Flood story (Manu was advised by a fish to build an ark). The world is governed by objective order—the law inherent in all things. The gods are only guardians of that law. The Brahmanas teach laws of sacrifice and that sacrifice is a periodic ritual by which the universe is re-created and regulated. The great sacrifice was the horse sacrifice.

After this came the *ARANYAKAS* which replaced physical sacrifice with teaching on physiological techniques like breathing control.

From the eighth century BC came the *UPANISHADS*. Early Upanishads taught that Brahman (God) was impersonal. Brahman was the inner essence of the world, the underlying reality. Even the gods were ignorant of Brahman.

Later Upanishads (especially the Svetasvatara Upanishad) taught that Brahaman is personal, the Great Lord. The gods were aspects of this one Great Lord. Brahman was personalized for a time as Brahma but he was replaced by Shiva and Vishnu.

The *BHAGAVAD GITA* (Song of the Lord) is the most important Hindu scripture. It describes a civil war which brings about the fourth age of deterioration before the gods destroy and re-create the world. A leading character is Arjuna, who hates war. The Bhagavad Gita is an account of a dialogue about war with his charioteer who is Krishna.

Krishna points out that death doesn't destroy the Atman. Each man must fulfil his caste duty. If he acts, even in war, with detachment he will not be guilty. Knowledge, work and devotion are all ways to salvation for all classes. Brahman is portrayed as a personal, loving God who becomes known as the atman through yoga.

Gods

The early Vedic Gods were Agni (god of fire), Indra (the war god, often depicted astride an elephant), Varuna (god of the cosmic order) and Rudra (the storm god).

Later gods include:

BRAHMA: creator, lord of all; depicted with four faces and arms, or as a swan or lotus.

VISHNU: preserver who controls human fate; depicted reclining on an ocean.

SHIVA: destroyer; opposites meet in him—good and evil, destruction and re-creation; king of the dancers (the dance is the rhythm at the heart of the cosmos and the individual); depicted with many hands, each pair symbolizing opposites; also depicted as the phallus or Lingam (male sexual organ); master of the yogis.

These three gods form the TRIMURTI, which has been described as the Hindu Trinity. But the concept is totally different from the Christian doctrine of the Trinity. Each of these gods has a consort:

Brahma has SARASVATI, goddess of knowledge and learning, and of the sacred river.

Vishnu has LAKSHMI, goddess of fortune and beauty.

Shiva has KALI (or DURGI), the Great Mother, a symbol of judgment and death. She is depicted as emaciated with protruding teeth and tongue, rolling eyes. She wears a garland of skulls and a skirt of severed heads. Yet she is also depicted as serenity who gives peace to her followers and inspires great devotion.

Avatars (incarnations)

Vishnu has ten avatars or incarnations, each for a different age in history. They are:

1. Matsya: the fish who warned of the Flood.
2. Kurma: the tortoise, rescued from the Flood and bearing the earth on its back.
3. Varaha: the bear who raised the earth from the Flood.
4. Nara-Simha: the man-lion who defeats demons.

5. Vamana: the dwarf who defeated the demons.

6. Parusha-Rama (Rama with an axe): he drove the sea back with an axe to reclaim the land, and defeated the warrior caste who theatened to take over the world.

7. Rama Chandra: hero of the Ramayana Epic. Rama Chandra, the epitome of virtue, was ousted from his throne for 14 years. His wife Sita was abducted to Sri Lanka. But Hanuman, the monkey god, formed himself into a bridge between India and Sri Lanka, so that she could be rescued.

8. Krishna: lover, warrior, king and a most popular god in his own right.

9. Buddha

10. Kalki: yet to come on earth, as a warrior on a white horse, to punish the wicked and reward the righteous. Kalki's incarnation will mark the end of the present age and the dawn of a new age in which Brahmanism will triumph.

Yoga

Yoga is intended to reverse the process of evolution and to return to the original unitary state. It is a means of delivering the whole soul to the deity. As one Hindu leader, Aurobindo Ghose put it, 'Yoga means union with the divine—a union either transcendental (above the universe), cosmic (universal) or individual or, as in our yoga, all three together.'

'The whole principle of yoga is to give oneself entirely to the Divine alone... and to bring down into ourselves by union with the Divine Mother all the transcendent light, power, wideness, peace, purity, truth-consciousness and Ananda of the Supramental Divine.'

There are eight stages:

1. Self control, restraint (*Yama*): includes truthfulness, chastity, non-violence, resisting acquisitiveness and stealing.

2. Observance (*Niyaama*): includes purity, content-

ment, austerity, reading the scriptures and devotion to the deity.

3. Posture (*Asana*): the well-known bodily actions.
4. Breath Control (*Pranayama*).
5. Withdrawal (*Prahyahara*): withdrawing the senses from awareness of the outside world.
6. Fixing Thoughts (*Dharana*): without the aid of the senses.
7. Meditation (*Dhyana*): attention stably directed to one point without distinction.
8. Ecstasy, Trance (*Samadhi*): no longer aware of even meditating. This may involve magical powers, levitation etc.

Tantrism

This movement involves goddess worship, dialogue with Shiva and his consort. The pupil is initiated by a guru with a mantra. A *mantra* is a single syllable which encapsulates energy and divine power. The utterance of the mantra evokes the power. It is the sound and meaning basic to the universe. A *yantra* is a visual mantra, ie a *mandala* (geometric diagram which leads the eye to a central point).

Tantrism, then, seeks to identify the worshipper with the deity with the help of a guru. Extensive parallels are drawn between the human body and the universe. There are usually six *chakras* (circles or centres) located along the spine. These are paralleled to mystical lines across the earth. The aim of meditation is to force the *kundalini* ('the coiled'), ie goddess power from the lowest chakra up the spine through each chakra then into the brain. This results in union with the divine.

Hindu worship

The BHAKTI MOVEMENT is a reaction to the yogis suppression of desire, love and feeling. It encourages a very emotional worship with weeping, excitement, hysteria, fainting and trances. The Bhagavad Gita depicts Krishna as encouraging bhakti worship towards himself.

TEMPLE WORSHIP will include PUJA (expressing respect and requests to God and offering food and water which is then shared by the worshippers). The worship will also include offering to statues of the gods, readings, prayers and mantras.

FESTIVALS include HOLI a spring festival to Krishna; DASARA an October festival to Kali; and DIVALI a new year festival.

Hindu leaders

A number of Hindu leaders have had significant influence in the West. Sri Ramakrishna (1836-1886) taught that all religions are true and he sought to combine Christianity with goddess worship.

Vivekenanda (1863-1902) was involved in the 1893 World Parliament of Religions. He formed the Ramakrishna Mission which stressed the universal significance of Hinduism as a religion able to absorb other religions. He influenced the Theosophical Society which spawned the New Age Movement. He taught that each person is potentially divine and needs to release the divine power within.

Ghandi (1869-1948) also encouraged the absorption of other religions into Hinduism.

Aurobino Ghose (1870-1950) had views similar to Vivekenanda, but he greatly influenced the West by writing in English.

Buddhism

Siddhartha Gotama (who became the Buddha) was born in Nepal in c.563 BC. He became deeply concerned about human suffering and out of this concern, Buddhism developed.

Beliefs

Buddhism is founded on natural truths taught in successive world ages (*kalpas*) each illuminated by Buddhas (enlightened ones). The fourth teacher for the present kalpa is Gotama Buddha.

The Buddhist aims at self-salvation which is seen as achieving enlightenment. Everyone has a latent Buddha-like faculty. The process is rational and intuitive. The only faith required is that where Buddha has trod, we may follow.

Buddhism differs from Hinduism mainly in rejecting the authority of the Vedas and Upanishads (although it accepts the Pali Suttas [scriptures]) and in denying the existence of individual souls.

The three universal truths

a. The Law of Change and Impermanence (*Anicca*): this states that all that exists—birth, growth, decay, death—are impermanent. They are part of an ever-rolling wheel. Nothing is permanent, everything is in flux. Only nirvana is permanent.

b. The Denial of the Soul (*Anatta*): there is no personal, immortal soul. Rather, all forms of life, including humans, are manifestations of the Ultimate Reality which is beyond change. So the whole of life is one and indivisible. The Ultimate Reality is indescribable (the 'Namelessness') because a God who could be described as having attributes could not be the final reality.

c. The Universality of Suffering (*Dukkha*): by suffering is meant everything which is unsatisfactory. This really includes the whole of life in this imperfect world.

Other beliefs

The universe was not created but evolved, and functions according to law (*karma*) not divine providence. Prayer to Buddha or a god cannot alter the law of karma.

Buddha taught that ignorance breeds desire; unsatisfied desire leads to re-birth and re-birth leads to further sorrow. It is vital therefore to eliminate ignorance so extinguishing desire and escaping re-birth and sorrow. This breaks the wheel of life (*Samsara*) (NB. Samsara includes more elements than ignorance, desire, re-birth and sorrow. In fact it has twelves 'spokes'—*nidanas*—which are beyond the scope of this outline).

Ignorance fosters the belief that re-birth is necessary, whereas it is possible to live a life which prevents re-birth. The desire to live as a real, distinct individual is the cause of re-birth. When this desire is removed the perfected individual through meditation enters Nirvana.

Ignorance (and sorrow) can be removed through knowledge of the Four Noble Truths. These are:

1. Suffering (*dukkha*) happens everywhere all the time. It is the result of karma.

2. Dukkha is caused by desire, greed and selfishness which can never be satisfied. Even desire for re-birth is selfish.

3. Desire can be overcome.

4. The way to overcome desire is through the Noble Eightfold Path. This consists of:

—*Right Views:* the Three Basic Truths; Four Noble Truths

—*Right Aims (Motive):* altruism.

—*Right Speech:*

—*Right Acts:* no killing, stealing, sexual immorality, lying, alcohol or drugs (ie. The Five Precepts).

—*Right Livelihood:* occupation compatible with the Noble Eightfold Path.

—*Right Effort:* strenuously preventing evil entering the mind; removing evil already in the mind, developing a good mind.

—*Right Concentration:* mind development; mind control.

—*Right Meditation:* ie going beyond a trance or psychic ecstasy to awareness of 'the still centre of the turning world'.

In the higher stages of the path occult powers (*Iddhis*) may be expected. The Esoteric Tradition of Buddhism states, 'When our great Buddha—the patron of all adepts, the reformer and codifier of the occult system—

reached first Nirvana on earth, he became a planetary spirit, ie his spirit could at one and the same time rove the interstellar spaces in full consciousness, and continue at will on earth in his original and individual body.'

Nirvana

Nirvana is the extinction of the limitations of selfhood. 'Through the destruction of all that is individual in us, we enter into communion with the whole universe.'

Schools of Buddhism

There are different forms of Buddhism.

Theravada Buddhism

This school adheres strictly to the *Pali Canon*. They chant the scriptures but do not pray. There are no gods, saviours or priests. The emphasis is on self-reliance. Buddhahood is attained by strict observance of the rules. Compassion towards humans and animals is stressed. Theravada Buddhism is found in Sri Lanka, Burma, Thailand and Cambodia.

Mahayana Buddhism

This school is not so bound by the Canon and tends to absorb other beliefs. Buddhahood is regarded as latent within each person. It merely needs developing. There is a greater emphasis on compassion.

An important difference is belief in *Boddhisattvas*, the saviours of mankind. A Boddhisattva is a Buddha who makes the supreme sacrifice and forgoes his rewards in order to transfer some of his merit to other lesser mortals. Faith is power in the power of Boddhisattva to save men from the consequence of ignorance.

The highest Buddha is Gotama Buddha. He is deified as the one historical manifestation of the eternal Buddha essence. He is supreme wisdom, the Ultimate and Only Reality. Secondly comes the Pratyeka Buddha—an independent private Buddha who has acquired and enjoys enlightenment. After this is the Boddhisattva followed by the Arhats. Below these is a pantheon of minor 'gods' (many from Hinduism) which are symbols of cosmic forces. The Boddhisattvas are the subjects of meditation, reverence and, in some cases, worship.

Pure Land School

This school dates from the fourth century AD. It believes in a Western paradise called the Pure Land (*Sukhavati*) in which believers will be gathered after death as a reward for faith and good works.

The teaching on Boddhisattvas is similar to the Mahayana School. There is a concept of original sin from which Boddhisattva can save people. The saviour of this school is Amida who vowed not to enter Buddhaland until all beings had. There is some stress on faith without works. All is put down to the grace of Amida Buddha. Even faith is the result of his grace.

Zen Buddhism

There is no concept of God, the soul or salvation. Scriptures, ritual and vows are not necessary, though some choose to use them.

Zen aims at a direct knowledge of reality ('Enlightenment' or *Satori*) which is beyond the intellect. Satori can only be described by silence. It is a foretaste of the Absolute Moment, of Cosmic Consciousness.

The potential for enlightenment is within everyone. This is achieved by two methods:

i. *Mondo:* very rapid, non-rational question and answers between master and pupil. The aim is to transcend thought. A typical question is 'What is the sound of one hand clapping?'.

ii. *Koan:* use of non-rational words or phrases.

All mental obstacles—thoughts and emotions—must be removed.

Tibetan Buddhism (Lamaism)

This is a deeply occult form of Buddhism with much sorcery and black magic. It believes there are in Tibet many 'spiritual masters'—humans who have attained Arhat and don't die but transfer their consciousness from life to life in successive bodies. They 'work on the inner planes of consciousness' communicating with enlightened human beings throughout the world. (Such teaching is behind Theosophy and influences the New Age Movement and occultism in the West).

Tibetans worship a very complex pantheon of gods with Adi Buddha as supreme. The Dalai Lama is regarded as a reincarnation of a Boddhisattva.

Islam

Muhammad

Muhammad was born in Mecca in c.571 AD. He had contact with Christianity, but probably an unorthodox form. It may be that he gained the idea that the Christian Trinity was God the Father, Mary and Jesus.

At the age of 40 he claimed the angel Jibrail (Gabriel) appeared to him and called him to proclaim the word of Allah and turn people away from polytheism. He was initially afraid, fearing that he might be possessed by evil spirits. But eventually he obeyed. His polytheistic neighbours rejected and persecuted him and his followers.

It is claimed that on one occasion he made a night journey to Jerusalem and ascended to heaven (from the site of the Dome of the Rock) to see Allah.

In 622, at Muhammad's command, the Muslims of Mecca emigrated to Medina. From the date of this journey (the *Hijrah*) the Muslim calendar began. Medina became the first Islamic state.

After numerous battles Muhammad and the Muslims returned to Mecca in 630. He died in 632.

Teachings

Islam means 'submission' and is a complete way of life. It has seven main beliefs which are divided into three groups:

*The Oneness of Allah (*Tawhid*)*

—*Allah:* He is the creator to whom the world belongs. He created it for the benefit of mankind. 'Say he is Allah, the One. Allah is Eternal and Absolute. None is born of Him, nor is He born. And there is none like Him.'

—*Predestination:* Everything is predetermined. Man is Allah's caliph (agent) who is free to obey or disobey God. He will be judged on the basis of intentions.

*Prophethood (*Risalah*)*

—*Prophets:* Some say there are 124,000 prophets. The Quran mentions 25: Adam, Enoch, Noah, Hud, Salih, Abraham, Ishmael, Isaac, Lot, Jacob, Joseph, Shuaib, Job, Moses, Aaron, Ezekiel, David, Solomon, Elias, Elisha, Jonah, Zechariah, John, Jesus and Muhammad.

—*Angels:* They were created from divine light. The most prominent are Gabriel, Michael, Azrail (angel of death) and Israfil (who will blow the trumpet at the Day of Judgment).

—*Books of Allah:* These include the Tawrat (Torah) of Moses, the Zabur (Psalms) of David, the Injil (Gospel) of Jesus [The apocryphal Gospel of Barnabas is regarded as the most reliable], and the Quran.

Muslims claim that the Quran ('reading' or 'recitation') is the only book still in its original, uncorrupted form. The Bible has been corrupted with false stories about the prophets (eg the lies of Abraham and Isaac; the drunkenness of Noah; the incest of Lot).

Muhammad said the Quran was revealed piecemeal to him over a period of 23 years by Jibrail and he memorised it. It is in 30 parts with 114 chapters (*surahs*) and 6236 verses.

Life after Death (Akhirah)

—*Life after Death.*

—*The Day of Judgment:* Islam believes in heaven and hell. Paradise is depicted as containing beautiful gardens, canals, young, beautiful girls, luxurious clothes, pearls, jewels, fruits, wine etc. Hell is depicted with fire, serpents, boiling water, extreme cold etc.

Other Beliefs

Doctrine of man

There is no original sin. Humanity is fundamentally good but not perfect, so needs reminding of the right paths. The worst sin is *SHIRK*, associating other gods with Allah.

Doctrine of salvation

Man does not need redeeming. God will forgive his sins.

Christology

Muslims greatly respect (even love) Jesus (*Isa*) as one of the great prophets. But he is not divine or the Son of God. 'It is not befitting to the majesty of Allah that he should beget a son.' The idea of incarnation compromises God's transcendence. In fact the Quran states that Jesus disclaimed deity (*Surah* 5:115-118). Islam accepts the virgin birth and miracles but not the crucifixion. God would not allow the Messiah to die a shameful death. The idea of Christ's sacrificial death is rejected by Islam. The Quran also omits Jesus' teaching from the Gospels.

Eschatology

Islam stresses eschatology. Jesus will return at the close of history to establish Islam throughout the world.

The Five Pillars of Islam

1. Declaration of Faith (Shahadah)

The fundamental creed of Islam is 'There is no god but Allah; Muhammad is Allah's messenger'.

2. The Five Compulsory Daily Prayers (Salah)

These must take place within set periods of the day or night:
 a. Fajr: dawn to just before sunrise.
 b. Zuhr: noon to afternoon.
 c. Asr: late afternoon to just before sunset.
 d. Maghrib: after sunset until daylight ends.
 e. Isha: night until midnight or dawn.

Islam emphasizes cleanliness so there are ritual ablutions before prayer. Then there is the Call to Prayer:

> 'Allah is the Greatest! (said four times)
> I bear witness that there is no god but Allah (twice)
> I bear witness that Muhammad is the messenger of Allah   (said twice)
> Rush to prayer! (twice)
> Rush to success! (twice)
> Allah is the greatest (twice)
> There is no god but Allah.'

When they pray, Muslims face Mecca and use various bodily actions, moving hands, standing, bowing, prostrating etc, and they recite from the Quran as well as praying.

3. Welfare Contribution (Zakah)

Muslims give a proportion of their wealth to help the needy, to win hearts to Allah and to gain merit with him.

4. Fasting (Sawm)

Muslims fast from dawn to sunset every day of Ramadan which is a month of forgiveness, mercy and a means of avoiding hell.

5. *Pilgrimage* (Hajj)

Those who can afford it will make a once in a lifetime pilgrimage to Mecca to walk seven times around the Kabah. The Kabah is a one storey cube-like building said to have been built by Adam but rebuilt by Abraham and Ishmael.

(Jihad, often translated 'holy war', means 'to try one's utmost'. Jihad means using all one's energies and resources to establish Islam and gain Allah's favour.)

The Sunni—Shia Division

90% of Muslims are Sunni. They believe that no-one could succeed Muhammad because the Quran said he was the final prophet. When Muhammad died the community elected four 'rightly-guided caliphs'—Abu Bakr (died 634); Umar (died 644); Uthman (died 656) and Ali (died 659).

The Sunnis gradually developed the Sharia Law, but the caliphate was replaced in 1924 by the governments of Muslim states.

10% of Muslims are Shia. They believe Muhammad appointed an imam who could give authoritative, infallible interpretation of the Quran. The first imam was Ali. Most Shiites believe the 12th imam (who guides the doctors of law—*ayatollahs*) will return as the Messiah.

Other aspects of Islam

Economics

It is forbidden to make money from alcohol, gambling, dishonesty or immorality etc. Interest is also banned but most Muslim countries accept a fixed rate of interest on bank deposits or from stocks and shares.

Marriage

A Muslim man may marry a Jewess or Christian but not a polytheist. But a Muslim woman may not marry a non-

Muslim. Women are highly esteemed and have property rights, freedom of earnings, rights of inheritance and the right to divorce a husband. A woman may defy her husband, father or brother if they ask her to go against the commands of Allah. Polygamy is allowed.

Food Laws

Similar to those in the Old Testament. Lawful food is called *Halal* (the equivalent of kosher).

Judaism

Jewish Holy Books

1. Tanakh (Hebrew Bible)

This is what we call the Old Testament. It consists of:

    a. the *Torah* (Pentateuch);

    b. the *Neviim* (Former prophets: Joshua—Kings; Latter prophets: Isaiah, Jeremiah, Ezekiel, 12 Minor Prophets)

    c. the *Ketuvim*: writings.

But it is important to realize that Judaism is not just based on the 'Old Testament'.

2. Midrash

A biblical commentary dating from the 3rd to 11th centuries AD.

3. Targum

A paraphrase of the Tanakh.

4. Talmud (Oral Law)

This was written down by 200 AD but includes much older material passed down orally through the centuries. It includes:

    a. *Mishnah* which contains *Halakah* (binding rules and

legal decisions) and *Haggadah* (less binding moral teaching, theology and legends).

b. *Gemara* a commentary on the Mishnah compiled between 200 and 500 AD.

5. Other Books

These include the Apocrypha (14 or 16 books, 11 of which were incorporated into the Vulgate); Apocalyptic (20 books from the 2nd to 1st century BC) and the Dead Sea Scrolls. The oral law continues to develop today.

Beliefs

Judaism is more concerned with behaviour than beliefs, so it tends not to have credal statements. The main creed is the Shema: 'Hear, O Israel, the Lord our God, the Lord is one.' However an historic summary of Jewish beliefs from the 12th century AD is found in:

The Thirteen Principles of Maimonides

Some of these will be recognized as formulated in reaction to Christianity.

1. There is only one creator who is omnipotent and omnipresent.
2. The creator is a unity. The Hebrew word in the Shema is *ehad* which can be a composite unity (eg used of marital union or of Israel). But Maimonides uses *yahid* which means a simple, absolute unity.
3. The creator is not a body and has no form.
4. The creator is first and last.
5. We must pray only to him.
6. All the words of the prophets are true.
7. Moses is the chief of the prophets.
8. The whole law was given to Moses.
9. The law will not be changed or replaced.
10. The creator knows everyone's thoughts and deeds.

11. The creator rewards those who obey the commandments and punishes those who don't.
12. The Messiah will come.
13. The resurrection of the dead.

Different traditions

In the main, this outline is describing traditional, orthodox Judaism. But other traditions include:

Liberal/Reform (or Progressive)

They have a liberal view of scripture and sit light to the oral law. Their emphasis is on the prophets. They use the vernacular language; do not observe food laws and avoid sex discrimination.

Conservative

These represent a move back towards orthodoxy.

Reconstructionism

This largely American tradition emphasizes individual freedom and regards Judaism as simply one tradition amongst others. God is seen as abstract.

Mystical

The *Kabbalah* is a mystical tradition that has existed since biblical times. It combines magical practices with theological and mystical speculation particularly on the basis of numerology. It also teaches reincarnation. The most famous book from this tradition is the Zohar which dates from the 13th century. Most Jews in the mystical tradition today belong to the Hasidim sect.

Hasidim

This extreme Orthdox movement was founded by Baal Shem Tov, an 18th century East European who had 'miraculous powers'. The Hasidim manifest ecstatic joy, stimulated through loud chanting, strong bodily movements and dancing. They stress the ready forgiveness of God rather than the seriousness of evil.

Among the Hasidim the Zaddik is a 'perfectly righteous' individual who has freed his mind from distraction and concentrated on God in prayer. Ordinary mortals are encouraged to attach themselves to a Zaddik who can redeem them. In order to do this the Zaddik has first to mix with evil people and even descend to their level in order to raise them to a higher state. Some are known for their great devotion, others for their psychic and 'miraculous' powers.

Jewish festivals

Judaism centres on the home rather than the synagogue. The Sabbath meal and the Passover are important traditions celebrated in the home.

However the synagogue plays an important part too, as the House of Study, the House of Prayer and the social centre.

The Jewish year is shaped by various festivals:

—*Passover* which celebrates the exodus from Egypt and the wilderness wanderings.

—*Shavuot* (Pentecost) which celebrates the giving of the Torah. It is also one of Israel's harvest festivals marking the end of the grain harvest.

—*Rosh Ha Shanah*—the civil new year in Israel, a reminder of both creation and the Day of Judgment.

—*Yom Kippur* (Day of Atonement) which includes a 25 hour fast and an emphasis on repentance.

—Sukkot (Tabernacles) when families build a temporary shelter from branches etc, reminding themselves of the temporary homes in the wilderness wanderings. Sukkot is another harvest festival and marks the completion of the harvest.

—*Hanukah*—the feast of lights commemorating the re-dedication of the Temple after its defilement by Antiochus Epiphanes in 168 BC.

—*Purim*—which commemorates the deliverance of the Jews through Esther.

Judaism and Christianity

There are numerous differences between the two:

1. Judaism believes in one God in unity and prays directly to God. Christianity believes in one God in Trinity and prays through Christ.

2. Judaism believes in original virtue rather than original sin. It holds that people can choose between a good inclination and a bad inclination which are inherent to human nature.

3. Judaism accepts the divine authority of Rabbinic literature as well as the Hebrew Bible (OT).

4. Judaism believes that the Messiah or Messianic Age is yet to come. Christianity believes he has come and will return. Only truly orthodox Jews believe in a personal Messiah, a super-human as opposed to divine person. The Talmud on rare occasions speaks of a suffering Messiah but not one suffering for the sins of others. The Messiah will fully rehabilitate Israel in its ancient land and the restored Israel will bring about the spiritual regeneration of the whole of humanity.

5. Judaism has less emphasis than Christianity on the life after death. Most Jews only accept the immortality of the soul rather than the resurrection of the body.

6. Judaism stresses deeds rather than beliefs. The righteous of all nations will attain salvation. Sins can be atoned for by prayer, good deeds and especially repentance.

7. Judaism at best regards Jesus as a minor prophet.

Differences between the religions

Some people glibly claim that we are all worshipping the same God. Pluralists claim that the different religions are merely portraying culturally-conditioned 'different faces of God'. But it is evident that there are fundamental differences between the major religions.

Doctrine of God

Theravada Buddhists do not believe in a monotheistic God, nor do Zen Buddhists. Some Hindus believe in an impersonal Ultimate, others in many gods. Islam and Judaism share with Christianity a belief in monotheism. But this is fundamentally contradictory to the Buddhist and Hindu beliefs just mentioned.

Doctrine of Sin

In Hinduism and Buddhism the fundamental problem is not sin but ignorance. If people only knew the nature of Ultimate Reality they would be released from the cycle of rebirth. In Islam sin is more weakness than fundamental corruption. Judaism does not share the Christian view of original sin. Again there are important differences, fundamental in the case of Hinduism and Buddhism.

Doctrine of Salvation

Buddhists teach escape from Samsara to Nirvana by the Noble Eight-Fold Path. This is the path of discipline (the elimination of desire) and meditation (being enlightened as to the nature of Ultimate Reality). Pure Land Buddhism teaches salvation as primarily re-birth in the Pure Land after death. This is achieved by the grace of Amida Buddha through faith. But there is no concept of atonement.

Hindus teach a similar release by similar means to those taught in Buddhism or by devotion to a personal lord (bhakti).

Islam basically teaches salvation in paradise for those who keep the will of Allah. Judaism emphasizes right behaviour rather than beliefs and sees salvation basically through obedience to Yahweh. Both Islam and Judaism explicitly reject the need for atonement and, therefore, the atoning death of Christ.

The differences between Christianity and the other religions over the doctrine of salvation are fundamentally incompatible.

Doctrine of Christ

Some Hindus have been impressed with Jesus as a teacher. They may hold that God was in him as in Rama, Krishna etc.

A similar view is held by some Buddhists. The Christ spirit or Buddhic Principle overshadowed and indwelt Jesus, as other religious leaders.

Islam greatly respects Jesus as a great prophet, but ignores his teachings in the Gospels. Judaism, at best, regards him as a minor prophet.

None of the other religions regard him as the unique Son of God incarnate, as he himself claimed to be. Their views are fundamentally incompatible with his and therefore with Christianity.

Conclusion

It seems obvious that many of the basic truth claims of the various world religions are fundamentally incompatible. Consequently pluralism seems untenable.

APPENDIX 4 | PENAL SUBSTITUTION IN SCRIPTURE

The idea of penal substitution, that Christ bore the wrath of God against human sin, has been attacked for various reasons:

1. It is said to represent God as an angry tyrant who demands restitution.

2. It is said to divide the Trinity, setting the Father and the Son into opposition.

3. It is said to encourage a purely objective, mechanical view of redemption which is quite separate from any subjective change within the believer.

4. It is said to be unethical because it involves the innocent bearing the punishment of the guilty.

However it is necessary to see what Scripture actually teaches before addressing those questions. Dr Leon Morris, *The Apostolic Preaching of the Cross* (Tyndale Press: London, 1960)[1] has done a detailed linguistic study of the teaching on the Atonement in Scripture. This appendix relies heavily on Morris' thesis. But numerous other scholars are quoted too. The reader is referred to Morris' book for a detailed treatment of the subject and the controversy surrounding it. His work is widely respected and quoted by other scholars and commentators.

We shall look at the concepts of Redemption, the Wrath of God, Propitiation, Reconciliation and Curse.

The meaning of redemption

The concept of REDEMPTION is conveyed by *lutron* ('ransom'—see Matthew 20:28; Mark 10:45 etc.) and its associated word group together with words connected with the concept of purchase like *agorazo* and *peripoieo*.

The *lutron* word group fundamentally involves 'release by payment of a ransom price' (p10). This is very clear in non-biblical Greek.

a. Septuagint (LXX)

Lutroo occurs 99 times in the LXX translating either the Hebrew *g'l* ('to redeem, act as a kinsman') or *pdh* ('ransom by the payment of a price'). Morris comments that wherever *g'l* is used with a human subject a ransom price is involved and 'the idea of a substitute is basic to *pdh*.' (p14f)

Lutron translates *kopher* ('ransom price') on six occasions. A man whose ox gored another man forfeits his life but can redeem it by paying a *kopher* (Ex 21:28ff). Similarly the first born who belong to God are redeemed by the half shekel *kopher* (Ex 30:12). In Isaiah 43:3-4 Egypt and other nations are given in exchange for Israel, a substitutionary ransom price or *kopher*.

Morris comments, 'The LXX usage is such as to leave us in no doubt that *lutron* and its cognates are properly applied to redemption by payment of a price, and though the idea of price might fade when God is the subject, it never disappears.' (p20).

b. Post-Old Testament

Post-OT Jewish writers continued the same usage of the word. Both in classical authors and in common speech the words of the *lutron* group 'were closely associated with the redemption of prisoners of war, the release of slaves and similar processes... Nobody, writing to a group of Gentile Christians, could overlook associations that would inevitably be evoked by the terminology used' (p22f).

APPENDIX 4: PENAL SUBSTITUTION IN SCRIPTURE 197

c. New Testament

Lutron is used in Matthew 20:28 and Mark 10:45 to described Christ's death. In the Marcan passage the phrase used is that Christ gave his life as *lutron anti pollon* ('ransom for many'). In both the classics and *koine* Greek *anti* has the meaning 'in place of', 'instead of'. In the LXX Abraham offered the ram *anti* Isaac (Gen 22:13); Judah offered to stay in Egypt *anti* Benjamin (Gen 44:33); The Lord takes the Levites *anti* the firstborn (Num 3:12); Archelaus reigned *anti* Herod (Mt 2:22); God won't give a serpent *anti* a fish (Lk 11:11). Only on rare occasions does *anti* not mean substitution and these are exceptions not the rule (p30f).

d. NT Commentators

The substitutionary nature of the atonement as taught in Matthew 20:28 is affirmed by Dr Craig Blomberg, *'Matthew', The New American Commentary* (Broadman: Nashville, 1992), p308; F D Bruner, *'Matthew' vol.2* (Word: Dallas, 1990), p736; Dr R H Gundry, *Matthew— A Commentary on his Literary and Theological Art* (Eerdmans: Grand Rapids, 1982), p404; R C H Lenski, *Interpretation of St Matthew's Gospel* (Lutheran Book Concern: Colombus, Ohio, 1932) and Dr R T France, *'Matthew'* (Tyndale NT Commentaries: Leicester, 1985), pp293f.

Similarly the substitutionary meaning of *lutron anti pollon* in Mark 10:45 is affirmed by Dr C E B Cranfield, *The Gospel according to St Mark* (Cambridge University Press: London, 1959), pp342ff; D Edmond Hiebert, *Mark: A Portrait of the Servant* (Moody: Chicago, 1979), p261; Dr J A Brooks, *'Mark', New American Commentary* (Broadman: Nashville 1991), pp170f. F Buchsel, *Theological Dictionary of the NT* (Grand Rapids, 1964), says that *anti* means 'in place of' rather than 'to the advantage of'.

For a conclusive defence of the authenticity of Mark 10:45 see Cranfield, Brooks and V Taylor, *The Gospel according to Mark* (Macmillan NT Commentaries: London, 1952), p446.

So there is no reason to doubt that Mark 10:45 describes Christ's death in substitutionary terms.

Lutroo is used of the atonement in Titus 2:14 and 1 Peter 1:18-19. In the latter passage redemption through the blood of Christ is paralleled and contrasted with redemption through silver or gold. This is substitutionary.

Apolutrosis is a rare word outside the NT but it is used ten times of the atonement in the NT. It means 'release by payment of ransom'. The word is used of the atonement in Eph 1:7,14; Col 1:14 and Rom 3:24.

Sanday and Headlam, *The Epistle to the Romans*, International Critical Commentary (T & T Clark: Edinburgh, 1960), p86, comment on Romans 3:24, 'In view of the clear resolution of the expression in Mark 10:45 (Mt 20:28)... and in 1 Timothy 2:6... and in view also of the many passages in which Christians are said to be "bought", or "bought with a price" (1 Cor 6:20, 7:23; Gal 3:13; 2 Pet 2:1; Rev 5:9: cf Acts 20:28; 1 Pet 1:18-19) we can hardly resist the conclusion that *lutron* retains its full force, that it is identical with [the Greek word] *time* and that both are ways of describing the death of Christ. The emphasis is upon the *cost* of man's redemption. We need not press the metaphor yet a step further by asking (as the ancients did) to whom the ransom or price was paid.'

1 Timothy 2:6 declares that Jesus, the mediator, gave himself as *antilutron* for all. Morris translates this as 'substitute-ransom' and adds, 'The thought clearly resembles that of Mark 10:45, i.e. that Jesus has died in the stead of those who deserved death. If the thought of substitution is there, we find it here to an even greater degree in view of the addition of the preposition which emphasizes substitution.' So also Professor G W Knight, *The Pastoral Epistles* (Eerdmans: Grand Rapids, 1992), pp121f.

The wrath of God (Romans 1:18)

C E B Cranfield, *The Epistle to the Romans*, International Critical Commentary (T & T Clark: Edinburgh, 1975), p108f, comments on Romans 1:18, 'What is meant by *orge theou*? Dodd has argued that by this phrase Paul did not mean to indicate a personal reaction on God's part but "some process or effect in the realm of objective facts", "an inevitable process of cause and effect in a moral universe". But when he says, "we cannot think with full consistency of God in terms of the highest human ideals of personality and yet attribute to Him the irrational passion of anger", he is begging the question by assuming that anger is always an irrational passion. Certainly it sometimes is; but there is also an anger which is thoroughly rational. That Paul would attribute to God a capricious, irrational rage is more than improbable. But a consideration of what Dodd calls "the highest human ideals of personality" might well lead us to question whether God could be a good and loving God, if He did not react to our evil with wrath. For indignation against wickedness is surely an essential element of human goodness in a world in which moral evil is always present.'

Professor J R Edwards, *Romans*, New International Bible Commentary (Hendrickson: Peabody, Mass., 1992), p48f, makes a similar comment, adding, 'Wrath and righteousness... are equally expressions of God's grace. If in what follows we hear the gavel of condemnation, it is only to hush all human protestations and self-justifications so that the acquittal of grace may be heard. The judge condemns *in order to* save.'

Professor Douglas Moo, *Romans 1-8*, The Wycliffe Exegetical Commentary (Moody: Chicago, 1991), p94, agrees and quotes Nygren as saying, 'As long as God is God, He cannot behold with indifference that His creation is destroyed and His holy will trodden underfoot. Therefore He meets sin with His mighty and annihilating reaction.'

John Ziesler *Paul's Letter to the Romans* (SCM:

London, 1989), p74f, says 'Dodd allowed too little weight to the connection, both in Jewish tradition and in Paul, between the wrath and the Day of Judgment... As God is indubitably the Judge, it is unlikely that Paul saw the wrath, even in its present operation as in this passage, entirely in impersonal terms.' He adds,'The wrath of God is not a matter of God's emotions, as if he were in a state of chronic ill-temper with humanity, but is rather something like his constant pressure against evil of every kind.'

H Wheeler Robinson writes, 'This wrath of God is not the blind and automatic working of abstract law—always a fiction, since "law" is a conception, not an entity, till it finds expression through its instruments. The wrath of God is the wrath of divine Personality.' *Redemption and Revelation* (London 1942), p269, quoted in Morris, *op.cit.*, p166

Morris (*op. cit.*), p131, points out that there are twenty words expressing the wrath of God in the OT and over 580 occurrences of these words. Also Jesus taught the wrath of God. (See Mt 5:22; 18:8; 25:41,46; Mk 3:29; 9:43-48; Lk 12:5; 13:3,5; 21:23; Jn 3:36; cf Mt 8:12; 11:20,24; 13:42, 50; 18:34; 21:44; 22:7, 13, 33; 24:51; 25:30; Mk 14:21; Lk 13:28). Morris comments (*op.cit.*), p163f, 'In view of all this it is difficult to maintain that Jesus had discarded the conception of the wrath of God. For Him the divine reaction in the face of evil was a solemn and terrible reality.'

He points out that the wrath is specifically said to be of God in John 3:36; Rom 1:18; Eph 5:6; Col 3:6; Rev 19:15 cf Rev 11:18; 14:10; 16:19. Then there is 'the wrath of the lamb' in Rev 6:16. 2 Thess 1:7-9 vividly associates wrath with Jesus as he returns in the parousia.

Propitiation or Expiation?

In Romans 3:25 it says God presented Christ as *hilasterion*. Does this mean propitiation (removing God's wrath) or merely expiation (cleansing from sin)?

The word comes from the *hilaskomai* word group.

APPENDIX 4: PENAL SUBSTITUTION IN SCRIPTURE 201

Morris points out that there is general agreement that in non-biblical Greek this means 'propitiation' or 'appeasement' (*op.cit.*), p126.

Concerning the LXX, he says,'It may well be that, on occasion, the best word with which to render *hilaskomai* is "forgive" or "purge"; but if the particular forgiveness or purging of sin is one which involves, as a necessary feature, the putting away of divine wrath, then it is idle to maintain that the word has been eviscerated of all idea of propitiation. Dodd totally ignores the fact that in many passages there is explicit mention of the putting away of God's anger...' (*op.cit.*), p138.

Morris continues (p155), 'No sensible man uses one word when he means another and in view of the otherwise invariable Greek use it would seem impossible for anyone in the first century to have used one of the *hilaskomai* group without conveying to his readers some idea of propitiation.

Professor Moo (*op.cit.*), p.237, states, 'the conclusion that *hilasterion* includes reference to turning away God's wrath is inescapable.' Commenting on Romans 3:25, John Zeisler (*op.cit.*), p113, says, 'Dodd's argument is vulnerable, as there are places where we do seem to find propitiation in the sense of that which averts the divine wrath... We cannot rule out all notion of propitiation here in any dogmatic fashion.' (Nevertheless he believes it is difficult to extract from this verse the idea that God is being placated by Jesus death).

However Professor Matthew Black *Romans*, New Century Bible (Oliphants: London, 1973), p72, says, 'The context in Romans supports the sense of "propitiation": both the immediate and remoter context (eg.1:18) are concerned with the wrath of God.' Cranfield (*op.cit.*), p216, translates *hilasterion* as 'a propitiatory sacrifice'. Professor James R Edwards agrees that it is propitiatory (*op.cit.*, p105, as does Karl Barth, *The Epistle to the Romans*, transl. E C Hoskyns (Oxford University Press:

London, 1933), p105. See also James Dunn below on Romans 5:10.

Sanday & Headlam (*op.cit.*), p94, comment 'Following the example of St.Paul and St.John and the Epistle to the Hebrews we speak of something in this great Sacrifice, which we call "Propitiation". We believe that the Holy Spirit spoke through these writers, and that it was His Will that we should use this word. But it is a word we must leave to Him to interpret.'

In 1 John 2:2 Jesus is called *hilasmos*. Professor Raymond E Brown, *The Epistles of John*, Anchor Bible (Doubleday & Co: New York, 1982), p220, comments, 'Overall...it seems that there are connotations both of expiation and propitiation in the *hilasmos*-related words.' He quotes M Black as saying, 'the idea [of propitiation] is one that is repellent to the modern mind; yet it is central to the beliefs of the primitive church.' (*op.cit.*, p222)

Professor J L Houlden, *A Commentary on the Johannine Epistles* (A & C Black: London, 1973), p62, states, '*Hilasmos*, which we have translated by the general term "sacrificial offering", may well carry the more specific idea of "propitiation", and its associations with the term *parakletos* ['advocate' in 1 John 2:1]...confirms the presence of that idea here. Both images carry the idea of winning over the party to whom appeal is made or sacrifice offered.'

A E Brooke, *The Johannine Epistles*, International Critical Commentary (T & T Clark: Edinburgh, 1912), p28, comments on 1 John 2:2, '[Christ] is not only the High Priest, duly qualified to offer the necessary propitiation, but also the propitiation which He offers. The writer's meaning is most safely determined by reference to the Old Testament's theories of sacrifice, or rather of propitiation.'

Even C H Dodd says concerning this verse, 'in the immediate context it might seem possible that the sense of "propitiation" is in place.' *The Johannine Epistles*, Moffat NT Commentary, p26, quoted in Morris, (*op.cit.*), p178

Morris argues (p183ff) that those who reject the idea of propitiation seldom face the question why expiation is necessary. He says that expiation only has meaning in the context of personal relationships. Sin and guilt are not *things* which can be objectively removed. He adds that unless we believe in the wrath of God we empty God's forgiveness of its meaning.

The nature of Reconciliation

Sinful human beings are enemies of God according to Romans 5:10; Colossians 1:21 and James 4:4. The idea of reconciliation is conveyed in the NT by the *katallassein* word group.

Romans 5:10 states that we are reconciled (*katellagemen*) to God. But is this reconciliation only one-sided: our being reconciled to God? Or is God also reconciled to us?

Cranfield, *The Epistle to the Romans*, (*op.cit.*), p267, comments, 'The enmity which is removed in the act of reconciliation is both man's hostility to God...and also God's hostility to sinful man (this aspect of it is particularly clear in 11:28), though the removal of God's hostility is not to be thought of as involving a change of purpose in God.'

Professor James D G Dunn, *Romans 1-8*, Word Biblical Commentary (Word: Dallas, 1988), p260, comments on Romans 5:10, '...recognition of a harmony between the concepts of reconciliation and sacrifice, and that either can be used to speak of the turning away or ending of divine wrath (3:25 as the answer to 1:18-3:20; 5:9-10), should also discourage a revival of the view that it is only man who needs to be reconciled and not God; because God is the reconciler he does not cease to be judge.'

Morris quotes Handley Moule as saying that *katallage* and its cognates 'habitually point to the winning rather the pardon of an offended king, than the consent of the rebel to yield to his kindness.' *Outlines of Christian Doctrine* (London, 1892), p79, quoted in Morris (*op.cit.*), p209.

Sanday & Headlam (*op.cit.*), p130, state, 'We infer that

the natural explanation of the passages which speak of enmity and reconciliation between God and man is that they are not on one side only, but are mutual.'

Morris adds (p220) 'We cannot say that God was reconciled by any third party; rather He must be thought of as reconciling Himself. Even to say that Christ reconciled God does not give us the true picture; for it suggests a disharmony in the Godhead and also raises a doubt as to the constancy of God's love. But we must insist that God's love for us remained unchanged throughout the process of reconciliation.'

Christ—cursed for us

Galatians 3:13 states that, 'Christ redeemed us from the curse of the law by becoming a curse for us.'

Professor F F Bruce, *The Epistle of Paul to the Galatians*, NT Greek Commentary (Paternoster: Exeter, 1982), p165f, comments that Paul, 'Omits "by God" after *epikataratos* ['cursed'] in v 13 (contrast the LXX *kekateramenos upo theou* [Deut 21:23]...to avoid the implication that Christ in his death was cursed *by God*. This implication would conflict with Paul's conviction that Christ's enduring the cross was his supreme act of obedience to God (cf Rom 5:19) and that "in Christ God was reconciling the world to himself" (2 Cor 5:19). Paul leaves the question, "By whom was Christ cursed?" unanswered; what he does make plain is that the curse which Christ "became" was his people's curse, as the death which he died was their death.' (So J B Lightfoot, *St Paul's Epistle to the Galatians* [Macmillan & Co: London, 1890], p140)

He continues, 'Since the Messiah, almost by definition, enjoyed the unique blessing of God, whereas a crucified person, according to law, died under the curse of God, the identification of the crucified Jesus with the Messiah was a blasphemous contradiction in terms...When Paul was compelled to recognize that the crucified Jesus, risen from the dead, was Messiah and Son of God, he was faced with the problem how and why he nevertheless died under the divine curse. The solution set forth in vv 10-13 probably came to him sooner rather than later: Christ had endured the curse on his people's behalf (by being "hanged on a tree") in order to redeem them from the curse pronounced on those who failed to keep the law.'

Dr R Y K Fung, *The Epistle to the Galatians* (Eerdmans: Grand Rapids, 1989), p150, comments, 'Verse 13... represents Christ's death as a vicarious bearing of the curse of the law which delivers his people from the same curse.' So also Professor H N Ridderbos, *The Epistle of Paul to the Churches of Galatia* (Eerdmans: Grand Rapids, 1956), pp127f.

Professor C E B Cranfield, *The Gospel according to St Mark (op.cit.)*, pp458f, comments on Jesus' cry of dereliction in Mark 15:34, '...the cry is to be understood in the light of xiv.36, II Cor.v.21, Gal.iii.13. The burden of the world's sin, his complete self-identification with sinners, involved not merely a felt, but a real abandonment by his Father. It is in the cry of dereliction that the full horror of man's sin stands revealed.... (It is, of course, theologically important to maintain the paradox that, while this God-forsakenness was utterly real, the unity of the Blessed Trinity was even then unbroken.)'

Why the Cross was necessary

Romans 3:25 says that Christ's death was 'to demonstrate [God's] justice, because in his forbearance he had left the sins committed beforehand unpunished...'

Leon Morris comments (*op.cit.*), pp254ff, 'Classical Protestantism has understood this to mean that Christ bore the penalty of our sin, and that God in this way showed that the eternal law of righteousness cannot be allowed to suffer disrepute. Calvin puts it thus: "As the law allowed no remission, and God did remit sins, there appeared to be a stain on divine justice. The exhibition of Christ as an atonement is what alone removes it."... This kind of interpretation has been vigorously assailed, but it does appear to give the gist of the apostle's point... This is admitted by such a theologian as Hastings Rashdall, although his own view of the atonement is so very different, for he says: "St Paul does not quite say why God could not remit the penalty of sin without the death of His Son. But it cannot be denied that those theologians who declare that this would be incompatible with God's justice—the justice which requires somehow that sin should be punished—or with the consistency which demands the infliction of the particular punishment which God had threatened, namely death—are only bringing out the latent presuppositions of St Paul's thought." ' (*The Idea of the Atonement in Christian Theology* [London, 1925], pp91f)

Morris continues, 'It is objected to this interpretation that the bearing of penalty by one in the place of another is not really just, so that when Christ suffers for us it is not a matter of fulfilling legal requirements. There is some force in this objection, and there would be more if we were dealing with human law. But the fact is that we are not. The law in question is the law of God's holy nature, and that nature is merciful as well as just.'

He adds (p269ff) 'God is...a God of law...His forgiveness can be only such as is consonant with the law of His holy nature...We cannot expect God to make light of the moral demand when he deals with the situation posed by man's sin. It would be no answer to the needs of the situation for the Creator to say, "It does not matter. I freely forgive." P T Forsyth puts it strongly when he says that God "could not trifle with His own holiness. He could will nothing against His holy nature, and He could not abolish the judgment bound up with it...God's law is His own holy nature. His love is under the condition of eternal respect. It is quite unchangeable" ' (*The Work of Christ* [London, 1948], pp112f)

In this context Morris does a study of Justification which 'is a legal term indicating the process of declaring righteous' (p271). So Sanday & Headlam (*op.cit.*), p30. (See Morris, [*op.cit.*], pp224-274, for his study on justification and pp108ff for a study of the meaning of the word 'blood' concerning the atonement which he concludes refers primarily to sacrificial death).

Morris concludes his study with the important statement, 'Substitution, as we see it in the atonement, is not some purely external thing, which stops when it sees the wages of sin borne by the Substitute, but something which only reaches its consummation when the sinner comes to view sin with the same mind as his Substitute' (p280). Justification cannot, except for the sake of theological discussion, be separated from union with Christ and the reception of the Spirit. A person claiming justification, whose life shows no transformation into the likeness of Christ, is self-deceived.

Conclusion

In conclusion we may answer the four questions posed at the beginning of this Appendix.

1. God's anger is not the rage of a tyrant but a necessary reaction of One who is holy when confronted with sin (see above on 'The Wrath of God' on p.127ff).

2. Collaboration rather than division within the Trinity is conveyed in the NT as the plan of salvation is carried out (see Morris p220, F F Bruce pp165f and C E B Cranfield on Mark 15:34 all quoted on pp203-204).

3. There is nothing mechanical about redemption as the sinner needs to view his sin in the same way as his Substitute (see the last quotation from Morris above).

4. The innocent bearing the punishment of the guilty cannot be said to be unethical if it is a free choice of the Son of God in harmony with the nature and will of the Trinity. (See the section 'Why the Cross was Necessary' above).

[Space forbids looking at the whole idea of sacrifice in the OT being fulfilled in the sacrifice of the Lamb of God, eg. John 1:29; 1 Cor 5:7.]

Note

1. The current edition of the book is as follows: *The Apostolic Preaching of the Cross* by Leon Morris, Third Revised Edition, copyright 1965 Tyndale Press. Published in the USA by William B. Eerdmans Publishing Company.

APPENDIX 5 | **1 PETER 3:19-20; 4:6**

There are numerous interpretations of 1 Peter 3:19. Martin Luther commented, 'A wonderful text is this, and a more obscure passage perhaps than any other in the New Testament, so I do not know for a certainty just what Peter means.' The main views are as follows:

1. The pre-incarnate Christ preached through Noah to his wicked contemporaries (who are now spirits in prison)

Professor E P Clowney, *The Message of 1 Peter*, Bible Speaks Today (IVP: Leicester, 1988), p162f, quotes with approval Grudem's translation of the passage, 'He went and preached to those who are now spirits in prison when they disobeyed formerly when God's patience was waiting in the days of Noah.' Clowney comments, 'This preferred translation shows that the disobedience was going on along with the preaching. It is a perfectly natural expression if Peter is thinking of Christ's preaching through Noah.'

However I H Marshall, *1 Peter*, NT Commentary Series (IVP: Leicester, 1991), p126f, disagrees with Grudem's contention that the participle used without an article after the noun demands his translation. He points out that 'the force of the participle is ambiguous. It could be causal or temporal. If it is temporal, it could equally well be translated 'when or after they had formerly disobeyed'. Since the participle is aorist rather than present, this translation is the more probable, since the aorist participle usually (though not always) expresses an action preceding the time of the main verb.'

H B Masterman, *The First Epistle of Peter* (Macmillan:

London, 1900), p175, gives a more detailed linguistic refutation of this view.

C E B Cranfield, *The First Epistle of Peter* (SCM: London, 1950), p85, describes this interpretation that Christ was preaching through Noah as 'far-fetched'.

Professor Charles Bigg, *Epistles of St Peter and St Jude*, International Critical Commentary (T & T Clark: Edinburgh, 1902), p162, comments, 'There can be no doubt that the event referred to is placed between the Crucifixion and the Ascension. We must therefore dismiss the explanation of Augustine, Bede, Aquinas, and others, that Christ was in Noah when Noah preached repentance to the people of the time.'

2. An emendation of the text should be made so that the person who went and preached is Enoch, not Jesus

The contention is based on the similarity between part of the Greek text and the name Enoch. The Greek reads *en ho kai tois en phulake pneumasi poreutheis* (literally 'in which also to the in prison spirits having gone'). It is claimed that 'Enoch' should have been included after *en ho kai* but, because of the similarity of sound between the name and that phrase, it was accidentally omitted by a scribe. In the Book of Enoch 12 and 13, Enoch is said to have been sent down from heaven to announce judgment on the sinful angels of Genesis 6:2.

Cranfield, *op.cit.*, p84, comments, 'We may safely reject Rendell Harris' ingenious conjectural emendation of the text, which introduces Enoch as the subject of 'went and preached', although Moffat and others accepted it. A reference to Enoch would be quite irrelevant here.'

Professor E Best, *1 Peter*, New Century Bible (Oliphants: London, 1971), p139f, points out that there is no textual evidence in any manuscript for this view. He adds, 'Christ is the subject of verse 18 and again of verse 22 and a sudden transference of attention to Enoch does not suit the stream of thought.' E G Selwyn, *The First*

Epistle of Peter (Macmillan: London, 1946), p197f, agrees, calling the emendation 'celebrated but most improbable'.

3. After his death, Jesus went and preached to the spirits of Noah's human contemporaries who rejected his message of repentance

Variations on this view are:

   a. Jesus preached condemnation to them.

   b. Jesus preached only to those who were righteous.

   c. Jesus preached only to those who had been disobedient but repented in the hour of their death.

   d. Jesus preached the gospel to those who had been righteous and condemnation to those who had been wicked.

   e. Jesus preached the gospel (giving the opportunity of repentance) to the whole generation which was proverbially wicked. This shows the mercy of God.

Bigg, *op.cit.*, p162, considers that the 'spirits... were those of the men who refused to listen to Noah. *Pneumata* may be used of men after death (Heb 7:23), and the *nekrois* of 4:6 fixes this as the right sense. The *euaggelisthe*, again, of 4:6 must be taken to prove that in St Peter's view our Lord preached the gospel to these spirits, and offered them a place of repentance.'

He continues, 'The thought that underlies St Peter's words is that there can be no salvation without repentance, and that there is no fair chance of repentance without the hearing of the gospel. Those who lived before the Advent of our Lord could not hear, and therefore God's mercy would not condemn them finally till they had listened to this last appeal.' (So Clement of Alexandria Strom. vi. 6. 48). 'Thus St Peter does not here contemplate the case of those who have actually heard the gospel and refused it...'

Bigg then alludes (p163) to a similar idea in various Jewish writings which may have influenced Peter, namely the Book of Enoch and the Bereschit Rabba. He concludes, 'St Peter limits this Jewish doctrine to the special case of those who have not heard the gospel on earth.'

Cranfield, *op.cit.*, p85, accepts the view that Christ preached the gospel (in the normal sense) to the Flood generation. 'These would be mentioned as being generally regarded as the most notorious and abandoned of sinners: if there was hope for them, then none could be beyond the reach of Christ's saving power.'

(See below under view 4 for further comments relevant to this view.)

4. That, after his death, Jesus went and preached to the fallen angels who rebelled against God and married human women during Noah's time (see 2 Pet 2:4; Jude 6)

The 'sons of God' in Gen 6:2-4 are regarded in this view as angels. The phrase is used of angels in Job 1:6; 2:1. The preaching was probably a condemnatory declaration of victory. The word 'preached' is *ekeruxen* (a general word for proclamation) rather than *euaggelizo* (to preach the gospel).

Professor W J Dalton, *Christ's Proclamation to the Spirits*, Analecta Biblica (Pontifical Biblical Institute: Rome, 1965), p148, comments, 'It seems reasonable to maintain that New Testament usage strongly favours the meaning of "spirits" in the sense of superhuman beings.'

Professor P H Davids, *The First Epistle of Peter, New International Commentary on the NT* (Eerdmans: Grand Rapids, 1990), p139, writes that, ' "Spirits" in the NT always refers to nonhuman spiritual beings unless qualified (as, e.g., in Heb 12:23; see Matt 12:45; Mk 1:23,26; 3:30; Luke 10:20; Acts 19:15-16; 16:16; 23:8-9; Eph 2:2; Heb 1:14; 12:9; Rev 16:13,14).' He adds, p140, that normally deceased human beings are referred to as ' "souls" (*psuche*), not as "spirits" (*pneuma*).'

Michaels, *op.cit.*, pp208ff, agrees but asks why would Christ be so interested in events that happened three millenia ago. He favours the view that it is not the evil angels of Noah's day but their offspring. According to

1 Enoch 15:8-10 the disobedient angels united with human women in Gen 6 and the resultant offspring were the demons which, for example, opposed Christ in his earthly life. To overcome the difficulty that these demons are clearly not imprisoned he translates *phulake* not as 'prison' but as 'refuge'. He claims *phulake* is ambiguous like the English word 'security'.

Marshall, *op.cit.*, pp125f, regards Michaels' translation as 'very dubious'. He adds that Michaels 'offers it largely because the spirits are still active rather than restrained. But this overlooks the possibility that only one group of spirits is under restraint while others are still active.' He agrees, p127, that the spirits may have been the offspring of the above-mentioned angelic-human union.

Dalton, *op.cit.*, p150, points out that the fundamental meaning of the verb *kerusso* (translated 'preached' by the NIV in 1 Pet 3:19) is 'to act as a herald'. It does not necessarily mean to preach the gospel (in the normal sense). In the LXX translation of Jonah 1:2, Jonah is called to make a proclamation (*keruxon*) in Nineveh. This was a message of doom. Dalton concludes that the message preached in 1 Peter 3:19 is also one of doom. (So Davids, *op.cit.*, p141, and Selwyn, *op.cit.*, p200).

Dalton continues, p155, that the context of 1 Pet 3:19 is victory of Christians over their persecutors not the conversion of the lost. Hence verse 19 is likely to speak of victory over Christ's enemies rather than the salvation of lost spirits. He adds, p158, 'Nowhere in biblical literature is the world of the dead called *phulake*...On the other hand, *phulake* is used in the New Testament for the prison in which Satan is chained' (Rev 20:7).

Other reasons are given by Dalton for rejecting the idea that evangelism with the opportunity for repentance is meant by 1 Pet 3:19. He points, p159, to Matt 25:41 which leaves 'little room for this sort of conversion sermon; both the angels' fall and the earthly behaviour of men have irrevocable and eternal consequences.'

Selwyn, *op.cit.*, pp199f, comments, 'I cannot doubt that

the primary reference [of 1 Pet 3:19] is to... supernatural beings; but Enoch's descriptions of the wicked dead as well as fallen angels being bound in prison makes it possible that the former also were included in St Peter's mind, if not in the phrase itself.'

Professor F W Beare, *The First Epistle of Peter* (Blackwell: Oxford, 1947), p146, agrees. So does B Reicke, *The Disobedient Spirits and Christian Baptism* (Ejnar Munksgaard: Copenhagen, 1946), p90, because *pneumata* is used of both humans and angels in Jewish literature, and because humans are constantly linked with angels in sin and punishment.

But Dalton, *op.cit.*, p149, responds that these arguments are inconclusive. Nor has any example of such a usage of the word been offered.

Reicke, *op.cit.*, pp122ff, seeks to defend the idea of the fallen angels being redeemed. He refers to Rom 14:9 about Christ being Lord of both the living and the dead, which does not seem at all conclusive. In fact the context seems to be referring only to Christians. Secondly he refers to Eph 1:10 (all things being ultimately brought under Christ).

Dalton, *op.cit.*, pp188f, writes, 'Neither text is explicit enough to base a theory which goes against firm Christian tradition and which at the same time is out of harmony with the rest of St Paul's thought.' He adds that 2 Cor 15:24f speaks of all Christ's enemies ultimately being put under his feet, not redeemed.

The Meaning of 1 Peter 4:6

Masterman, *op.cit.*, p143, writes, 'This has been described as the most difficult text in the Bible. Indeed, some commentators have abandoned all hope of arriving at a satisfactory exegesis.' N Hillyer, *1 & 2 Peter, Jude, New International Bible Commentary* (Hendrickson: Peabody, Massachusetts, 1992), p122, comments, 'No fully satisfactory explanation of this verse has ever been given.'

1. The dead are the spiritually dead

This was the view held by Augustine, Cyril, Bede, Erasmus, Luther, etc. But it is rejected by the commentators quoted above on 1 Pet 3:19. They all say that 'dead' in this verse must have the same meaning as in the previous verse, referring to the physically dead. (See Blenkin, p94; Clowney, p175; Dalton, p267; Davids, p153; Marshall, p137; Masterman, p143 and Selwyn, p214.)

2. That the dead are only the generation of Noah, as in 3:19

For objections to this view see below.

3. The dead are all the dead

Beare, *op.cit.*, p156, strongly supports this view, arguing that the word 'dead' must be as all-embracing as in the previous verse. He writes, 'It is quite inadmissible to take it as meaning only those who have lived and died since the coming of Christ, and have heard the Gospel preached in their lifetime.' [So Best, *op.cit.*, p156; Davids, *op.cit.*, p154, and G W Blenkin, *The First Epistle General of Peter* (Cambridge University Press, 1914), p94.]

Bigg, *op.cit.*, pp170f, comments, '*Nekrois* [the dead] must be taken in the obvious sense of the word; they were dead at the time when the announcement was made. Further it must have the same sense as in *zontas kai nekrous* [the living and the dead], that is to say, it must include all the dead, not merely those who perished in the Flood'.

Dr William Barclay, *The Letters of James and Peter*, Revised Edition, The Daily Study Bible (The Saint Andrew Press: Edinburgh, 1976), pp248f, agrees with Bigg and concludes, 'In some ways this is one of the most wonderful verses in the Bible, for, if our explanation is anywhere near the truth, it gives a breath-taking glimpse of a gospel of a second chance.'

Cranfield, *op.cit.*, p91, comments, '... the most natural

interpretation is surely to connect it with 3:19, and to understand a reference to "the spirits in prison".'

However Marshall, *op.cit.*, pp136f, points out 'the insuperable obstacle with this view...it does not explain what the function of the verse is in its context.' Verse 5 refers to persecutors being condemned at the judgment. For the idea of the dead hearing the gospel and being saved to be taught in the next verse is illogical.

4. The dead are those who heard and accepted the gospel before they died

This interpretation is supported by the majority of the commentators on 1 Pet 3:19 quoted above.

Dalton, *op.cit.*, p270, asks, 'Is there anything harsh or repugnant in the interpretation: "For this is why Christ was preached to those who have since died..."? On the contary, given a proper appreciation of the context, it seems a reasonable, even the sole reasonable interpretation.'

Marshall, *op.cit.*, pp138f, comments, 'The one real objection to this view is the suggestion that it is unnatural to take "the gospel was preached to the dead" in the sense "the gospel was preached [in their lifetime] to those who [having subsequently died] are now dead." In its favor is that only on this view does the verse make sense in the context. It draws the required contrast between the fate of persecutors and those whom they persecute.'

Selwyn, *op.cit.*, p214, writes, 'It is tempting to see here a reference to the universality of Christ's judgment corresponding to the universality of His redemption...but no such reference is required by the text. It is simpler, indeed, to suppose that St Peter in verse 5 had in mind past and present members of the Church, and in verse 6 the first of these only.'

He adds, p339, 'The very reason why Christians–even those who were already dead–had had the Gospel preached to them was that, whatever the world may say of their troubled and seemingly fruitless lives here on earth, they might live eternally after God's likeness in heaven.'

The NIV translates this as 'the gospel was preached even to those who are now dead' but admits that the word 'now' is not in the Greek. The NIV Study Bible explains that 'it is necessary to make it clear that the preaching was done not after these people had died, but while they were still alive. (There will be no opportunity for people to be saved after death; see Heb 9:27.)'

(See also Clowney, *op.cit.*, p175; Hillyer, *op.cit.*, p122; and Michaels, *op.cit.*, p237, for support for this view.)

We conclude that:

a. Both verses are the subject of different interpretations. It is most unwise therefore to be too dogmatic, let alone build upon them an important doctrine of a second chance which is not taught elsewhere in Scripture, and which is contrary to the general teaching of Scripture.

b. In our view the most likely interpretation is that 1 Peter 3:19 refers to Christ's proclamation of judgment to the fallen angels and 1 Peter 4:6 the dead are Christians who heard the Gospel before they died.